The Collector's Cabinet

The Collector's Cabinet

Flemish Paintings from New England Private Collections

James A. Welu

Worcester Art Museum
Worcester, Massachusetts

This catalogue is published for the inaugural exhibition of the
Frances L. Hiatt Wing.
Exhibition dates: 6 November 1983–29 January 1984

ISBN: 0-87023-420-X
Distributed by
The University of Massachusetts Press
Post Office Box 429
Amherst, Massachusetts 01004

Library of Congress Catalogue Card Number: 83-50456

Designed by Helen Hadley
Typeset by Monotype Composition Company in Sabon and Palatino
Printed in the United States of America at Acme Printing Company, Inc. on
Lustro Offset Enamel Dull; 2,500 copies
Photography by Ron White
Project coordinator Gaye Brown

Cover illustration: *A Picture Gallery* (cat. no. 33) David Teniers the Younger.
Collection of Saul Steinberg
Frontispiece: *Port Scene in Venice* (detail; cat. no. 7) Jan Brueghel the Elder.
Collection of Mr. and Mrs. Robert Cushman

Foreword

The Worcester Art Museum celebrates this moment of renewal with an assertive bow to the past. This might be seen as something of a risk, but we believe that the values represented by both this catalogue and the exhibition it commemorates make it especially appropriate for us to do so.

The Collector's Cabinet is traditional in several key ways. It serves as a potent reminder of the museum's history of presenting important exhibitions of old master paintings, as well as of the significant collections we have in this field. The strength of that tradition shows up at certain points, such as the major exhibition of Flemish paintings we organized in 1939 with the Philadelphia Museum of Art and the more recent (1979) exhibit of Dutch paintings from New England private collections. In addition, *The Collector's Cabinet* focuses on the traditional role of the private collector/connoisseur, his relationship with and his importance to public museums such as ours. The exhibition also brings to public view and scholarly attention a number of previously unpublished and little-known works, thus adding significantly to our understanding of Flemish painting.

All of these are concerns deeply rooted in our history. In that sense, we still adhere to the values of the seventeenth-century critic Roger de Piles, who urged the study of great masters, a comparison of their works, and the examination only of originals when developing artistic standards.

But we celebrate herewith more than the art itself. In opening a new wing, the Worcester Art Museum is meeting the challenge of the future. That challenge is simply stated: the museum's commitment to *quality*—in collecting, exhibitions, scholarship, and education—can be no less than what it has been in the past. This community has long supported that challenge through large numbers of generous benefactors, notably Jacob Hiatt, whose special generosity has made possible both the Frances L. Hiatt Wing and this exhibition, which opens the wing's major gallery. We are grateful to Jack Hiatt for his support and leadership in this time of looking ahead. We are also grateful to our many lenders, without whom this exhibition would have been no more than a good idea. Finally, I am delighted to thank Chief Curator James A. Welu, organizer of the exhibition, who conceived of it and saw it through its many phases. Jim combines an extraordinary range of knowledge with a gentle modesty that somehow masks the drive it takes to accomplish this sort of task. But he has once again made clear the role of the curator as artist, presenting us with an exhibition that is itself a work of art.

Tom L. Freudenheim

Director, Worcester Art Museum

Acknowledgements

This exhibition and catalogue would not have been possible without the help of many individuals. I am particularly grateful to Jacob Hiatt, whose generous support of the entire project has been a key factor in its success.

The talented staff at the Worcester Art Museum has assisted me in so many ways. I would like to thank, in particular, Timothy Riggs for reading over the catalogue entries and offering many valuable suggestions, and also Gaye Brown for her fine editing and for overseeing the entire publication project. I am grateful to the museum's conservators, Paul Haner and David Findley, who did technical examinations and undertook conservation work on a large number of the paintings. I would also like to acknowledge Ron White for his photography and John Reynolds for his work on many of the frames. Other staff members who deserve special thanks are curatorial assistants Joanne Carroll and Sandra Petrie; registrars Stephen Jareckie and Sally Freitag; preparator Tom Keaney; education curator Martha Krom; librarians Kathy Berg, Anne Walsh, Peter Andrews, and Cynthia Bolshaw; typists Ethel Taubert, Holly Moir, Virginia Harding, and their supervisor, Bev Willson; publications assistant Roberta Waldo; and the entire maintenance staff for their help in mounting the exhibition. Our director, Tom Freudenheim, has been most encouraging and supportive of all of us in this collaborative effort.

Research for this project would not have been possible without the valuable resources made available to me at the Fine Arts Library at Harvard University, the Frick Art Reference Library in New York, the Rijksbureau voor Kunsthistorische Documentatie in The Hague, the Witt Library of the Courtauld Institute in London, the Rubenianum in Antwerp, the documentation center of the Louvre, and the library of Kunsthandel P. de Boer in Amsterdam. I am grateful for the kind assistance provided to me by the staff of these institutions, in particular Rupert Hodge, Marijke de Kinkelder, Gerbrand Kotting, Thea Lans, Charles Roelofsz, and Madelon Steinhauser.

In my research, I have benefited greatly from discussions with many colleagues and friends. I would like to especially thank Arnout Balis, Albert Blankert, Christopher Brown, Zirka Filipczak, Julius Held, Paul Huvenne, George Keyes, Cécile Kruyfhooft, Walter Liedtke, Henk Nalis, Otto Naumann, William Robinson, Sam Segal, Marc Vandenven, Hans Vlieghe, and Willem van de Watering.

Individuals who were very helpful in securing some of the loans are Bob Haboldt, Rodney Merrington, Clyde Newhouse, and John Walsh, Jr.

Special thanks go to Helen Hadley for her handsome design of the catalogue and poster and to Clifford La Fontaine for his well-conceived design of the exhibition installation.

Finally, I am most indebted to the private collectors whose paintings make up this exhibition. They have been extremely generous in not only lending to the show, but also providing access to the works for study and photography. It has been my interaction with these individuals that has enabled me to appreciate most of all the joys connected with the collector's cabinet.

Introduction

The title of this exhibition derives from the private art collections, or "cabinets," that came into vogue during the late sixteenth and seventeenth centuries. The term *cabinet*, which now usually refers to a piece of furniture, was then used to describe a small room frequently used for the display of objects. A collector's cabinet, however, might be as large as a gallery, depending on the size of the collection. These cabinets, which were created throughout Europe by members of the nobility and the rising middle class, became popular in Antwerp, the major Flemish art center at the time. Collectors' cabinets were often the subject of paintings by Antwerp artists, such as David Teniers's *Picture Gallery* of around 1670 (cat. no. 33). Whether actual or imaginary, these "painted cabinets" convey the enthusiasm for collecting that coincided with Antwerp's golden age of painting.[1]

a Frans Francken the Younger, Flemish, 1581–1642, *A Wunderkammer*, panel, 74 x 78 cm. Kunsthistorisches Museum, Vienna

The collector's cabinet, which the Flemish referred to as *konstkamer* ("art cabinet"), is in many ways ancestor to the art museum as we know it today. These cabinets developed out of a more general type of collection, known in Germany as the *Kunst- und Wunderkammer* ("cabinet of man-made and natural curiosities"). A painting by Frans Francken the Younger shows the eclectic nature of these cabinets (fig. a), the contents of which ranged from Renaissance sculpture to dried specimens of exotic fish. Such collections, which were as much the predecessor of the science museum as the art museum, were representative of the late medieval and Renaissance encyclopedic vision of the world. This vision had a strong influence on painting, especially still life. Detailed renderings of flowers, shells, butterflies, or man-made objects—anything worthy of interest or study—were valued as much for their subject as their skillful execution. A good example is Hendrik van der Borcht's *Collection of Ancient Objects* (cat. no. 5), which undoubtedly was once part of a curiosity cabinet, possibly the artist's own. Another painter greatly affected by these encyclopedic collections was Jan van Kessel, who, like his grandfather Jan Brueghel the Elder, often used them as a setting for allegorical or mythological subjects (cat. no. 21).

The transition from the *Wunderkammer* to the cabinet devoted primarily to the fine arts was a gradual one. An early example was that of the Antwerp merchant and connoisseur Cornelis van der Geest. Extremely active in the art world, he commissioned many contemporary artists and collected not only their work, but also art from the past. Willem van Haecht's celebrated painting of Van der Geest's cabinet (fig. b), dated 1628, gives an idea of the richness of the collection.[2] The proud owner stands among a group of people at the left pointing to one of his most important possessions, a *Madonna* by Quentin Massys, long considered the founder of the Antwerp School. Van Haecht's painting documents not only Van der Geest's collection, but also the social circles in which he moved. Seated at the left are Archduke Albert and Archduchess Isabella, who, like Van der Geest, commissioned many of the

b Willem van Haecht, Flemish, 1593–1637, *The Cabinet of Cornelis van der Geest*, 1628, panel, 99 x 129.5 cm. Rubenshuis, Antwerp

artists who are also present, including Rubens, to the right of the archduke, and Van Dyck, behind and to the left of Van der Geest. Van Haecht, who was charged with taking care of Van der Geest's collection, has been identified as the man about to enter the room at the far right.

Among the more distinguished visitors to the Van der Geest cabinet was the prince of Poland, Vladislaus Sigismundus, who stands to the right of Rubens, behind the upper left corner of Massys's *Madonna*. One of the numerous foreign collectors who acquired a large number of Flemish paintings, Vladislaus made many of his acquisitions during his visit to Antwerp in 1624. His cabinet, part of which appears in a painting by Etienne de la Hyre, included *Madonna and Child in a Floral Garland* by Hendrik van Balen and Jan Brueghel the Younger (cat. no. 1).

Although *Madonna and Child in a Floral Garland* is the only documented example, undoubtedly many other paintings in this exhibition were once included in *konstkamers*. Pieter Huys's *Woman Enraged* (cat. no. 20), for example, may well be the painting of "a screaming woman with a pot in her hand" that in the 1653 inventory of an Antwerp estate was listed as in a *konstkamer*.[3] The estate was that of Jeremias Wildens, one of the many Antwerp artists involved in collecting. Greatest of the artist-collectors was Rubens, whose cabinet included both ancient and contemporary art, including many examples of his own work.

One of the most important cabinets of the seventeenth century belonged to Archduke Leopold Wilhelm, governor general of the Southern Netherlands between 1647 and 1656. Born in Vienna and raised in Madrid, Leopold Wilhelm had the opportunity to study the collections of both Charles V and

c David Teniers the Younger, Flemish, 1610–1690, *Archduke Leopold Wilhelm in His Gallery in Brussels*, ca. 1651, canvas, 123 x 163 cm. Kunsthistorisches Museum, Vienna

Philip II. A voracious collector himself, the archduke brought a large number of Italian paintings with him to the Netherlands and there he continued to acquire works of art. Among the many Flemish artists he patronized was David Teniers the Younger, who served both as court painter and keeper of the collection. Teniers painted numerous views of the archduke's cabinet. Considered mementos, these paintings were often used by the archduke as a way of sharing his collection. Eventually Leopold Wilhelm returned to Vienna, where today his collection forms a major part of the Kunsthistorisches Museum.

One of Teniers's views of Leopold Wilhelm's cabinet is now in the Kunsthistorisches Museum along with many of the works represented in it (fig. c). The archduke, wearing a tall hat, stands to the left of Teniers, in front of a large portion of his Italian collection. The archduke's fondness for his Italian paintings resulted in his commissioning Teniers to paint small-scale copies of a large number of them. These copies were engraved and published in *Theatrum Pictorum*, one of the first illustrated catalogues of a collection. Many of these same paintings appear in Teniers's *Picture Gallery* (cat. no. 33), which was painted long after the archduke's collection went to Vienna. In this imaginary cabinet, the Italian paintings are taken out of their gold frames, given simple black moldings, and used as the background for a group of more prominently displayed Flemish paintings.

Teniers's highlighting of the Flemish works in *A Picture Gallery* suggests the pride in the Antwerp School that had been developing during the seventeenth century. The contributions to painting that had been made by Antwerp artists were demonstrated in the private collections that were formed at this time. They included not only a wide range of subject matter, but often works from different periods, as in Teniers's painting in which the *Madonna and Child* by Gossaert, one of the pioneers of the Antwerp School, is displayed next to one of Teniers's own, a scene of peasant merrymaking.

In many ways this exhibition is similar to a *konstkamer* of the late seventeenth century, for it represents a wide range of artists and subject matter. Here one can trace the development of different genres within the Antwerp school. Examples of still-life painting range from the sixteenth-century work by Joachim Beuckelaer, a pioneer in this area, to an eighteenth-century painting by Peeter Snijers. A similar historical range can be seen in portraiture, landscape, religious, and genre painting. Coming from twenty-three New England private collections, these works have rarely been exhibited in public. Thanks to the generosity of the owners, the Worcester Art Museum is able to offer a glimpse of the *konstkamer* of New England and demonstrate once again the richness and diversity of the Antwerp School.

---

1 The most complete survey on this subject to date is S. Speth-Holterhoff, *Les Peintres flamands de cabinets d'amateurs au XVIIᵉ siècle* (Brussels: Elsevier, 1957). See also Z. Filipczak's forthcoming book, *Art about Art: Antwerp, 1550–1700*. I am grateful to Zirka Filipczak for sharing with me her thoughts on this subject.

2 See J. S. Held, "Artis Pictoriae Amator: An Antwerp Art Patron and His Collection," *Rubens and His Circle: Studies by Julius S. Held* (Princeton: Princeton University Press, 1982), pp. 35–64.

3 The painting was located in the balcony of the *konstkamer* (*inde Const Camer opde gaelderye*). See J. Denucé, *De Antwerpsche "konstkamers" inventarissen van kunstverzamelingen te Antwerpen in de 16ᵉ en 17ᵉ eeuwen* (Amsterdam: De Spieghel, 1932), p. 167, no. 587. I would like to thank Julius Held for bringing this to my attention.

Hendrik van Balen 1575–1632
Jan Brueghel the Younger 1601–1678

1

Madonna and Child in a Floral Garland
Oil on copper, 41.8 x 32.4 cm

One of the hallmarks of seventeenth-century Flemish painting was the collaboration among artists. Painters often specialized in certain areas and combined their individual talents to produce a single work. In this painting, the figures can be attributed to Hendrik van Balen and the flowers to Jan Brueghel the Younger, two artists who are known to have collaborated in this way.[1] Both attributions are based on style and technique, and, as we shall see, on some specific species of flowers for which the younger Brueghel is known.[2]

Paintings incorporating elaborate floral garlands were popular in seventeenth-century Flanders. Often they include figures, usually a religious subject. The earliest examples were painted during the first decade of the seventeenth century by Brueghel's father, Jan the Elder, who also frequently collaborated with Van Balen. In these early works, the figures are usually confined to the center and treated as a separate unit, like a painting within a painting.[3] Here, by contrast, putti appear on all sides of the U-shaped garland. Close study suggests they were painted first and the flowers added later.

The number and variety of flowers that Brueghel incorporated in this garland is amazing. The botanist and art historian Sam Segal has identified more than 130 different species, including at least thirteen varieties of tulip, eleven of iris, and ten of anemone. Characteristic of the younger Brueghel are the barberry *(Berberis vulgaris)*, the small garden nasturtium *(Tropaeolum minus)*, and several wild species. These particular plants help distinguish the younger Brueghel's floral paintings from those by his father.[4]

While the detailed floral garland is indicative of an increasing interest in natural science, the religious subject it frames is a type of devotional image that was popular at the time. The Madonna and Child are surrounded by not only the garland, but also a colorful mandorla of light. Christ holds a bunch of grapes, symbol of the Eucharist, and the Madonna places her foot on a crescent moon. High above her head, four putti carry a gold crown with stars. This combination of symbols recalls the apocalyptic vision that by this time had become associated with the Virgin: "A woman robed with the sun, beneath her feet the moon, and on her head a crown of twelve stars" (Rev. 12:1).

When this work came to light a few years ago, nothing was known about its provenance. Its early history can be documented, however, because the painting appears in a still life by the French artist Etienne de la Hyre.[5] Painted in Warsaw in 1626, De la Hyre's still life shows part of the art collection of the Polish prince Vladislaus Sigismundus, including this work, which at the time

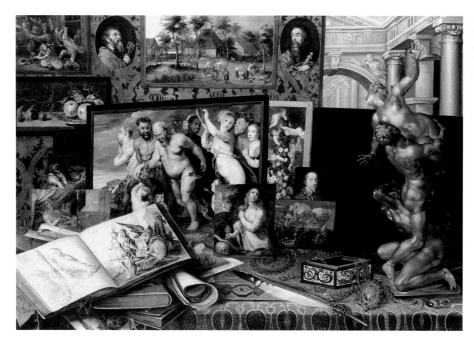

1a Etienne de la Hyre, French, 1583–1643, *The* Kunstkammer *of Prince Vladislaus Sigismundus Vasa,* 1626, panel, 72.5 x 104 cm. Private collection (photo: courtesy Heim, London)

had a narrow gold frame (fig. 1a). All the paintings in De la Hyre's still life are Flemish,[6] and they almost certainly were purchased or commissioned by the prince during his visit to Flanders in 1624.[7]

The date on De la Hyre's painting proves that *Madonna and Child in a Floral Garland* was completed by 1626. Since Jan Brueghel the Younger was not yet a member of the Antwerp guild when he left for Italy in 1622, it is unlikely he collaborated on the floral painting before that time. And since he was still in Italy when the Polish prince visited Antwerp in the fall of 1624, he could not have received a commission from him directly. In fact, the painting may have been a commission for Van Balen and Jan Brueghel the Elder, who undoubtedly was visited by the prince, but who died only a few months later on 12 January 1625. If so, the painting was probably one of the projects the younger Brueghel inherited when he returned to Antwerp later that year to take over his father's studio.[8]

Paintings like *Madonna and Child in a Floral Garland* were common in the art cabinets of the seventeenth century. It is easy to see how they would have appealed to the private collector, for they are collections in themselves, enabling the viewer to enjoy on an intimate scale the many beauties of the natural world.

Verso: Two stencils in black paint *659E; 9...D...*

Provenance: Prince Vladislaus Sigismundus Vasa, Warsaw, 1626; B & S Auction Service, Portland, Conn., 25 July 1976; private collection.

1 Other examples in this catalogue are nos. 15, 21, 25, 38. A painting that appears to be a copy of this work was sold in Paris on 21 June 1974 by Laurin-Guilloux-Buffetaud-Tailleur: no. 9, *La Vierge à la guirlande de fleurs*, panel, 43 x 33 cm. The painting was attributed to Jan Brueghel (the Elder) based on a 1956 letter from M.J. Friedländer, who noted that the figures were by another hand. In this painting, the Christ Child holds a pearl instead of grapes.

2 See: M.-L. Hairs, "Collaboration dans des tableaux de fleurs flamands," *La Revue belge d'archéologie et d'histoire de l'art* 26 (1957): 149–62.

3 See K. Ertz, *Jan Brueghel der Ältere...* (Cologne: DuMont, 1979), pp. 302–25.

4 Another distinguishing factor is the father's greater use of glazes. The younger Brueghel's floral paintings are discussed by M.-L. Hairs, "Jean Breughel le Jeune, peintre de fleurs," *Revue belge d'archéologie et d'histoire de l'art* 36 (1967): 57–74.

5 I am grateful to Zirka Filipzcak for calling this to my attention.

6 For a discussion of De la Hyre's painting and the identification of its contents, see J.A. Chrościcki's entry in *Objects for a "Wunderkammer,"* exh. cat. (London: P & D Colnaghi, 1981), no. 148, pp. 311–13. Chrościcki identified the floral garland painting as a work by Jan Brueghel II, but was referring to the work on panel cited in note 1 above. The latter, which appears to be a later copy, shows variations in the putti and the flowers, proving that it is not the work in the De la Hyre painting.

7 The prince's visit to Flanders was in connection with the siege at Breda. While in Antwerp, he visited the studios of well-known artists, including Rubens. For a summary of the prince's visit, see C. Buelens and M. Rooses, *Correspondance de Rubens...,* 6 vols. (Antwerp: Jos. Maes, 1887–1909), 3:306–7.

8 This was not the only connection between the younger Brueghel and the Polish prince. In 1632 Brueghel proposed to paint for Vladislaus, who was then king of Poland, a copy of a garland of fruit that was a collaborative work by his father and Rubens. See J. Denucé, *Brieven en documenten betreffend Jan Bruegel I en II* (Antwerp: De Sikkel, 1934), pp. 80–81.

Joachim Beuckelaer   *ca. 1535–1574*

2

Still Life, 1562
Oil on cradled panel, 73.9 x 106.5 cm

Beuckelaer was one of the pioneers in still life painting. Greatly influenced by his uncle and teacher, Pieter Aertsen, he concentrated on kitchen and market scenes with elaborate displays of food and household equipment. The secular nature of these paintings is usually offset by a biblical scene tucked into the background. In this painting, however, which is his earliest signed and dated still life,[1] Beuckelaer shows a genre scene in which several figures prepare food, while two others warm themselves at a fire.[2] These activities, combined with the types of food in the foreground, suggest that the theme of the painting is winter.[3] In the days before refrigeration, one could usually tell the season by the type of food on the table. Almost all of the provisions depicted here were traditionally eaten during winter: game, oranges and lemons, parsnips,[4] cabbages, winter carrots, and chestnuts.

The seasons were a popular motif in Netherlandish art and were usually depicted as a series of four separate works, most often landscapes. This painting may well have been one of four or perhaps paired with another picture suggesting summer. A search of Beuckelaer's known works, however, has failed to reveal any pendants.

In addition to food, the still life includes several containers for drink: in the center, an earthenware jug and at the left, a spouted pewter tankard, or *pypkan,* and two glasses. A variety of plates and baskets is used to display the viands to their best advantage. The ceramic dish at the right holds a piece of molded butter, which was a rather expensive item at the time.

Beuckelaer arranged his still life to give a strikingly close-up view of all the objects. The heavily laden table, which takes up most of the picture plane, appears to be part of the viewer's own space. Adding to this illusion is the way in which several items overlap the table's edge. These illusionistic effects are counterbalanced by numerous shifts in perspective that tend to flatten the picture space. The basket of cabbages and carrots is seen from the side, while the table is seen from above. Likewise, the left side of the table, which shows a change from the original design, does not line up with the back.[5] A similar distortion appears in the large, orange plate in the center, the left side of

which is on a different plane from the right. Such irregularities almost go unnoticed because of the extremely realistic rendering of the objects themselves.

The woman at the left, who holds a kettle and large skimming spoon, forms a transition both in color and scale between the life-sized objects in the foreground and the much smaller, monochromatic genre scene behind. This type of monumental female figure appears in many of Beuckelaer's kitchen and market scenes, often as the principal subject. The archway behind the woman links her visually to the still life and also frames the background scene. Its prominent keystone mask suggests Beuckelaer's architectural interests, which, as his paintings demonstrate, ranged from ancient to contemporary.[6]

In certain sections of the work, the underdrawing is visible, for the upper layers of paint have become transparent with age. Several of the sketch lines show that the artist departed from his original design, as seen at the upper right where the head of purple cabbage was originally larger. Infrared photography also shows more clearly that Beuckelaer originally intended a round object, probably another fruit, in the space just above the lemon.

In the end, Beuckelaer achieves a design that at first glance seems rather haphazard, but in fact contains a variety of geometric relationships, one of which is the placement of the four meats: in the center, the fowl and the side of meat, both on earthenware plates; and on either side, the duck and pair of rabbits, both on a stack of napkins. The two rabbits form a more obvious symmetrical design, one virtually a mirror image of the other.

It is interesting to note that one of the rabbits has a clipped ear (fig. 2a), a detail that probably relates to a hunting practice that was documented in *Jacht-Bedryff*, from about 1635.[7] In this manuscript we learn that the Dune Master, who leased sections of the dunes for hunting, clipped the ears of his mature female rabbits as a way of marking them so they would not be killed, thereby ensuring a continued population.[8] It is thus not surprising that Beuckelaer's painting is, if not the only, certainly one of the few still lifes to show this detail.

2a Detail of *Still Life*

Signed at upper right with monogram *IB;* dated on edge of table *1562.*

Provenance: Mrs. Joseph H. Beattie, Dobbs Ferry, N.Y., 1954; Coll. Mr. and Mrs. Julius S. Held.

References: K.P.F. Moxey, *Pieter Aertsen, Joachim Beuckelaer, and the Rise of Secular Painting in the Context of the Reformation* (New York: Garland Publishing, 1977), p. 100. Moxey, "The 'Humanist' Market Scenes of Joachim Beuckelaer: Moralizing Exempla or 'Slices of Life'?," *Jaarboek van het Koninklijk Museum voor Schone Kunsten Antwerpen,* 1976, pp. 167–68.

Exhibition: *Paintings and Sculpture from the Collection of Mr. and Mrs. Julius S. Held,* Smith College Museum of Art, Northampton, Mass., 1–27 October 1968, no. 13.

1 This still life was painted two years after Beuckelaer became a master in the Antwerp painters' guild. His earliest known works, which date from the preceding year, are figural compositions: *Market Women,* Kunsthistorisches Museum, Vienna, and two *Market Scenes with Ecce Homo,* one in the Nationalmuseum, Stockholm, and the other, now destroyed, formerly in the Gemäldegalerie Schleissheim, West Germany.

2 Moxey (1976 and 1977) misidentified the figures in front of the fireplace as Christ and His disciples at Emmaus. In fact, the figure to the right of the fireplace is a sculpture.

3 This was first proposed by Julius S. Held. For a discussion and illustrations of this theme in Netherlandish art, see E. van Straaten, *Koud tot op het bot: De Verbeelding van de winter in de zestiende en zeventiende eeuw in de Nederlanden,* exh. cat. (The Hague: Dienst Verspreide Rijkscollecties, 1977).

4 Parsnips, which today are extremely rare in the Netherlands, were once a main winter staple, especially before potatoes were introduced from the New World.

5 A pentimento shows that the left ledge was originally angled more to the right, which, perspective-wise, would have related better to the back edge.

6 See T. H. Lunsingh Scheurleer, "Pieter Aertsen en Joachim Beuckelaer en hun ontleeningen aan Serlio's architectuurprenten," *Oud-Holland* 62 (1947): 123–34; and Moxey, 1976 and 1977.

7 This manuscript by Cornelis Jacobsz. van Heenvliet is in the Koninlijke Bibliotheek, The Hague. See the modern edition by A.E.H. Swaen (Leiden: E.J. Brill, 1948), p. 22. I am grateful to Scott A. Sullivan for this reference.

8 The clipping of a single ear was the way in which female hares were protected in the early nineteenth century, according to F.A.J.C. Baron van Voorst tot Voorst, *Jagers-taal* (Arnhem: J.G. Meijer, 1838). For this reference, I am grateful to P. Tuijn, director of Het Nederlands Jachtmuseum.

Pieter van Bloemen 1657–1720

3

The Rest
Oil on canvas, 62 x 57 cm

3a Van Bloemen, *A Caravan,* 1704, canvas, 46 x 49 cm. Prado, Madrid

Pieter van Bloemen, who was born and studied in Antwerp, arrived in Rome in 1685, the same year as his younger brother Jan Frans. The two joined the *Schildersbent,* a fraternity of northern artists, and in accordance with the practice of the organization, Pieter received a nickname, "Standard," no doubt because of the banners that appear in his scenes of soldiers and encampments. Unlike Jan Frans, who remained in Italy the rest of his life, Pieter returned to Antwerp by 1694.[1]

Van Bloemen was especially skilled at painting animals and frequently added them to the works of other artists. In his own paintings, a white horse often plays a major role. Here, set against a dark background and dramatically lighted, it is the centerpiece in a beautiful arrangement of animals. The copper kettle strapped to its side provides a colorful note, echoed by the rust-colored calf. A turkey in the saddle faces the distance, where a shepherd tends some sheep.[2]

The Rest appears to have been painted somewhat earlier than another of Van Bloemen's caravan scenes, which is dated 1704 (fig. 3a). The latter shows the broader brushwork and more even lighting of the artist's later style, particularly in the treatment of the old man tending the horse. In the later work, a monkey replaces the turkey atop the horse, adding the same decorative note and suggesting that the variety of animals is even more important than the creation of a scene from everyday life. In a sense, Van Bloemen's menagerie is a veritable still life of livestock.

Signed lower right *PVB*

Provenance: Sale, Heilbron, Berlin, 30 September 1913, no. 8 (illus.); Mr. and Mrs. Louis Holzer, Brno, Czechoslovakia; private collection.

Exhibition: Belvedere, Brno, Czechoslovakia, February–March 1925, p. 44 (illus.).

1 The most extensive study on Van Bloemen is A. Busiri Vici, "Pieter van Bloemen detto 'Stendardo,'" *Studi romani* 8, no. 3 (May–June 1960): 279–87.

2 Sometime before 1913, the date of the earliest reproduction of this painting, the sky was completely overpainted; the addition was removed in a recent conservation treatment.

Theodor Boeyermans *1620–1678*

4

The Madonna Venerated by Saints
Oil on canvas, 54 x 39 cm

Boeyermans, an Antwerp artist, made this modello, or preparatory sketch, for a large painting of the same subject, which is still in its original location over the main altar of the Begijnhof Church in Malines, Belgium (fig. 4a).[1] Considering the number of commissions Boeyermans received during his lifetime, one can assume that he painted many modelli like the one shown here, but only one other is known today.[2]

The finished altarpiece, signed and dated 1672, measures over fourteen feet high. Both in subject and composition it recalls Rubens's altarpiece for the Church of the Augustine Fathers at Antwerp completed more than a half century earlier (fig. 4b). Like many of Boeyermans's paintings, the Malines altarpiece shows the strong influence that Rubens had on artists of the second half of the century.

Boeyermans takes a traditional Catholic theme, the Madonna and Child surrounded by saints, and uses its diverse cast of characters to create an extremely colorful and dramatic image. In the modello, the Madonna and Child and Saint Joseph appear on an elevated throne surrounded by numerous angels and saints, including the two patron saints of the church for which the final altarpiece was made, Saint Catherine of Alexandria and Saint Alexis.[3] Saint Catherine, who kneels before the Christ Child, receives the ring symbolizing her mystical marriage to Him, while a young angel behind her introduces another of her attributes, the broken spiked wheel. Saint Alexis kneels in the foreground holding a pilgrim's staff; a ladder on the ground next to him alludes to the stairs under which he spent his final days as a beggar. Behind him are Saint Charles Borromeo, dressed in his cardinal robes, and Saints Ursula and Agnes, who join hands while also holding their respective attributes, an arrow and a lamb. A sixth saint, Elizabeth of Hungary, stands at the far right. Dressed in royal attire, she holds two books and a triple crown. The sword and crown on the ground before her represent her royal birth, and the model of a church refers to Marburg, where she cared for the sick and needy.

The modello offers us a chance to see the artist at a more spontaneous moment. He virtually designs in color, using a variety of techniques to convey the final effect. To suggest the richly embroidered inner garment of Saint Elizabeth, he simply scrapes through the upper layer of dark green paint to reveal some of the more intense, red pigment beneath. In the upper part of the painting, vertical strokes of gray and a few touches of pink serve to represent the architectural background and the flowers scattered from above.

4a Theodor Boeyermans, *The Madonna Venerated by Saints,* canvas, 450 x 310 cm. Begijnhof Church, Malines (photo A.C.L., Brussels)

Boeyermans made several changes between his modello and the finished altarpiece.[4] The semicircular top of the final work prompted him to rearrange the group of angels overhead and, at the same time, expose more of the architecture. In the large painting, the figures on the upper level are placed higher and farther away from the viewer. The overall pyramid design is further strengthened by several changes in the foreground: Saints Ursula and Agnes are moved more toward the center, while Saint Alexis, who holds a ladder instead of a pilgrim's staff,[5] is given a slightly different pose farther to the left. The shift in Alexis's position is complemented on the right by the insertion of a small angel bearing the three crowns of Saint Elizabeth, who holds instead the model of a church. Centered at the bottom of this now more symmetrical design is the coat of arms of Sophie de Salazar, donor of the altarpiece.[6]

Changes were also made in the positions of the musical angels at the upper left (figs. 4c and 4d). The final placement of the lutist's right hand may have been dictated by contemporary music practice, for by the second half of the seventeenth century, the "thumb-under" technique, as seen in the modello, had long been replaced by the "thumb-out" technique, which appears in the final painting. The latter position was considered more elegant and reflects the period's emphasis on graceful gestures in court society.[7] Given that Boeyermans's Madonna is portrayed as a queen surrounded by a court of angels and saints, the musician's pose is particularly appropriate.

The finished altarpiece also shows some alterations in color, particularly in the use of red. The robe of Saint Charles, which in the final work takes up a greater area, is rendered a more vibrant red to better counterbalance the intense vermilion of Saint Elizabeth's robe at the right. Boeyermans also used red for the color of the drapery behind and over the arm of Saint Agnes, instead of the grayish tone seen in the modello. These changes, combined with the reduction of red drapery at the top of the painting, give greater weight and immediacy to the lower part of the composition and, at the same time, emphasize the exalted station of the Madonna and Child.

4b Peter Paul Rubens, Flemish, 1577–1640, *Enthroned Madonna and Child Surrounded by Saints,* 1628, canvas, 564 x 401 cm. Koninklijk Museum voor Schone Kunsten, Antwerp (on loan from Church of Saint Augustine)

Verso: Inscription on paper...*Leslie* (?) *Esq.;* label inscribed *7936/FH + S;* round label inscribed *91.*

Provenance: Sale, Savoy, N.Y., 13 November 1959, as by Van Thulden; Coll. Mr. and Mrs. Julius S. Held.

Exhibition: *Paintings and Sculpture from the Collection of Mr. and Mrs. Julius S. Held,* Smith College Museum of Art, Northampton, Mass., 1–27 October 1968, no. 14 *(Mystic Marriage of Saint Catherine).*

---

1 The altarpiece is designed so that the picture revolves to reveal a second painting, Lucas Franchoys the Younger's *Assumption of the Virgin,* which today is shown only for the feast

4c Detail of the modello *The Madonna Venerated by Saints*

4d Detail of the altarpiece *The Madonna Venerated by Saints*

of the Assumption. For discussions of Boeyermans's finished altarpiece, see M. Vandenven, "Theodoor Boeyermans, 1620–1678: Leven en kerkelijke kunst" (Ph.D. diss., Rijksuniversiteit, Ghent, 1975), pp. 105–7; M.-L. Hairs, "Propos sur quelques tableaux du XVIIe siècle," *Studia mechliniensia: Bijdragen aangeboden aan Dr. Henry Joosen...*, 1976, pp. 274–76; M.-L. Hairs, *Dans le sillage de Rubens: Les Peintres d'histoire anversois au XVIIe siècle* (Liège: Université de Liège, 1977), p. 255. I am grateful to Marc Vandenven for his comments on the Malines altarpiece.

2 The other modello, also on canvas (52 x 33 cm) and now in a private collection in Belgium, is a study for another altarpiece, *The Martyrdom of Saint Lawrence* (canvas, 300 x 180 cm) in the church at Heemskerk, The Netherlands. That modello was also once attributed to Van Thulden; see M.-L. Hairs, "Théodore van Thulden, 1606–1669," *Belgisch tijdschrift voor oudheidkunde en kunstgescheidenis* 34 (1965): 63, 64. The semicircular design at the top of the Heemskerk altarpiece does appear in the modello, unlike in this preparatory sketch.

Boeyermans's sketch, like the final work, is painted on canvas. Earlier in the century wood appears to have been the more common support for modelli. Almost all of those by Rubens, for example, were painted on wood (cat. no. 29). The use of canvas for preparatory sketches was even more common during the following century, as seen in the painting by De Roore (cat. no. 28).

3 Over-life-sized sculptures of both saints make up part of the elaborate marble framework that surrounds the finished painting.

4 The only other known modello by Boeyermans (see n. 2) also shows that the artist made changes in the finished work. Rubens, who completed at least four oil sketches for his Saint Augustine altarpiece, made many similar changes before arriving at his final design. See J. S. Held, *The Oil Sketches of Peter Paul Rubens: A Critical Catalogue*, 2 vols. (Princeton: Princeton University Press, 1980), 1: 519–22.

5 Greater attention to the ladder may have resulted from the artist's attempt to distinguish Saint Alexis from Saint James, whose most common attribute is a pilgrim's staff with a wallet or water-gourd.

6 Sophie de Salazar's (d. 1683) coat of arms consists of thirteen gold stars on a blue field.

7 The "thumb-out" technique was already being recommended in 1603 by the lutist Jean-Baptiste Besard. See J. Sutton, "The Lute Instructions of Jean-Baptiste Besard," *Musical Quarterly* 51 (1965): 345–62, esp. 355–56. I am grateful to Kenneth Bé for bringing this to my attention.

Hendrik van der Borcht

5

A Collection of Ancient Objects
Oil on copper, 25.7 x 21 cm

It is impossible to say whether the signature on this painting refers to Hendrik van der Borcht the Elder (1583–1660) or the Younger (1614–1665?).[1] Both were painters and engravers and both were interested in antiquities. The father was a connoisseur and collector of ancient objects whose expertise was admired by the great English collector Thomas Howard, Earl of Arundel. The younger Van der Borcht was also connected with Arundel; he accompanied the latter's agent, who was buying works of art in Italy, and later went to England, where he made engravings of Arundel's collection.[2]

This painting is one of three known still lifes by Van der Borcht. The largest and most elaborate is a circular painting in the Hermitage, Leningrad (fig. 5a); the other, a horizontal composition in the Historisches Museum, Frankfurt (fig. 5b).[3] All three feature antique items, many of which appear in more than one work. In each case the artist fills the picture plane with the objects, displaying them to their fullest advantage against a dark green background. Careful attention is also given to details such as inscriptions and the different colors and textures of the various metals and stones. Judging from the medals and coins, the objects appear to be reproduced in their actual size.

All of the medals and coins in the painting can be identified (fig. 5c).[4] Most are Greek and Roman, but at least two are Renaissance copies of ancient pieces, which can be identified because of Van der Borcht's extremely detailed rendering of their inscriptions. One (6) is an imitation of a bronze sestertius from the reign of Tiberius (fig. 5d),[5] the other (7) an imitation of a bronze medallion from the reign of Marcus Aurelius (fig. 5e).[6] Both copies are by the famous medalist from Padua, Giovanni da Cavino (1500–1570). These so-called Paduans were not originally designed as forgeries; by the time this still life was painted, however, many were being passed off as genuine antiques and were already in some of the most celebrated collections of Europe.

The bronze statuette of the urinating Hercules at the right may also be a Renaissance imitation of a classical piece, judging from its rounded forms and the color of the metal, which seems to be new. The same piece appears in the

5a Van der Borcht, *Still Life with Antiquities,* copper, 34.5 cm. Hermitage, Leningrad

5b Van der Borcht, *Still Life with Antiquities,* copper, 20 x 25 cm. Historisches Museum, Frankfurt

Leningrad painting. Another sculpture that may be a more recent work is the large figure of a seated female made of silver and gold, which can also be seen in the Frankfurt still life. This rather unusual piece may date from the late sixteenth or early seventeenth century. The two other sculptures include a marble torso of Aphrodite and a female bust, which can be identified as a bronze furniture mount of a type widespread in the Hellenistic and Roman worlds. The glass vessel and red, terra-cotta jar in the background appear to be Roman.

The still life also includes a variety of cameos grouped together at the lower left. The largest, a portrait of a man in a helmet, can be seen in the Leningrad painting as well. Three of the gems, including the large, double portrait, are also repeated in the Frankfurt still life. Although none can be identified with originals, they seem to be sixteenth- or seventeenth-century renditions in the classical manner.[7]

The three Van der Borcht still lifes appear to document a specific collection, which probably belonged to either the father or the son. They were not the only painters interested in antiquities; one of the greatest collectors of this period was Rubens, who assembled an important group of ancient sculptures and medals and whose collection of antique gems was among the finest of his day.[8] Such cabinets reflect the interest in antiquity that flourished during and after the Renaissance, when antique pieces were valued as works of art and as a way of learning about the past.[9]

Signed lower right on back of brooch(?) *HVBorcht*

Provenance: Dealer D. H. Cevat, London, ca. 1958; private collection.

Reference: *Peter Paul Rubens 1577–1640*, vol. 1: *Rubens in Italien, Gemälde, Ölskizzen, Zeichnungen*, exh. cat. (Cologne: Wallraf-Richartz-Museum, 1977), p. 232.

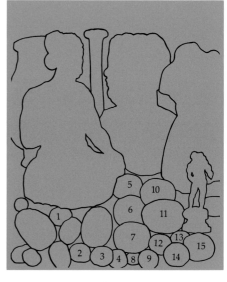

5c Coins and medals: 1. Greek silver coin, head of Zeus (?); 2. Greek gold coin of Lysimachus (obverse), head of Alexander, 3–2 cen. B.C.; 3. Roman gold coin, veiled head flanked by pontifical instruments (a *lituus* above a cup on the left and an *apex* on the right), *DIVVS (C)AESAR;* 4. Roman gold coin, head with laurel crown, *AVGVST(VS) DIVI·F;* 5. Roman bronze coin, head of a man; 6. bronze sestertius by Cavino, 16th cen. (reverse), *CIVITATIBVS AS(IAE RESTITVTIS)/S C;* 7. bronze medallion by Cavino, 16th cen. (reverse), *IMP VII COS III*, shield inscribed *VIC/AVG;* 8. Greek silver coin, head of Apollo (?); 9. Greek silver coin of Chalcis (reverse), ca. 196–146 B.C., eagle and serpent, *XAΛKI MENEΔ(H);* 10. bronze sestertius, Roman (reverse), *S C;* 11. Roman bronze medallion, A.D. 161–69 (obverse), head of Marcus Aurelius and Lucius Verus, *IMP ANTONI(N)V(S) AVG COS II* (sic) *IMP VERV(S) COS II;* 12. Roman gold coin (obverse), head of Vitellius, A.D. 69, *ΛVITELLIVS GERMANIC IMP…;* 13. gold coin, Greek or Roman, Athena or Roma; 14. Greek silver coin (obverse), head of Philip of Macedon; 15. Greek silver coin of Mithradates VI of Pontus (obverse), 120–63 B.C.

5d Giovanni da Cavino, Italian, 1500–1570, sestertius, bronze. Kunsthistorisches Museum, Vienna

5e Giovanni da Cavino, Italian, 1500–1570, medallion, bronze. Bibliothèque Nationale, Paris

1 For a discussion of the two artists and a list of known works, see E. Plietzsch, *Die Frankenthaler Maler* (Leipzig: E. A. Seemann, 1910), pp. 16–20.

2 Portraits of both artists and a poem on each are included in Cornelis de Bie's *Het gulden cabinet*... (Antwerp: J. Meyssens, 1661), pp. 127–28, 382–83. For the younger Van der Borcht's connections with Arundel, see F.C. Springell, *Connoisseur & Diplomat*... (London: Maggs Bros., 1963), pp. 100–104.

3 The Leningrad and Frankfurt paintings are discussed in *Stilleben in Europa*, exh. cat. (Münster: Westfälisches Landesmuseum, 1979), pp. 106–9. All three works are on copper.

4 For the identification of the medals and coins, I am grateful to G.K. Jenkins and I. Carradice of the British Museum.

5 Cavino's copy shows the *S C* on the reverse side rather than the obverse, as in the original.

6 Cavino's copy bears the number *III* after *COS* instead of *II*, as in the original. The obverse of this medallion, which shows a profile portrait of Marcus Aurelius, appears in the Frankfurt still life immediately to the right of the neck of the large head. Cavino engraved two obverse and two reverse dies of this medallion, which differ only slightly in workmanship. For a comparison, see Z.H. Klawans, *Imitations and Inventions of Roman Coins* (Santa Monica: Society for International Numismatics, 1977), pp. 92–93, nos. 2 and 3.

7 I am grateful to A.G. Somers Cocks of the Victoria and Albert Museum and J.D. Draper of the Metropolitan Museum of Art for their comments on the cameos.

8 Like the Van der Borchts, Rubens was familiar with other contemporary collectors of antiquities, in particular the French scholar Nicolas-Claude Fabri de Peiresc, with whom he planned to publish a study of the more important gems known at the time. The study was to be illustrated by engravings made after drawings by Rubens. See M. van der Meulen, *Petrus Paulus Rubens Antiquarius: Collector and Copyist of Antique Gems* (Alphen aan den Rijn: Canaletto, 1975), and O. Neverov, "Gems in the Collection of Rubens," *Burlington Magazine* 121, no. 916 (July 1979): 424–32.

9 See "Die Münze als Objekt des Sammeleifers und der numismatischen Forschung," in H. Maué and L. Veit, *Münzen in Brauch und Aberglauben*, exh. cat. (Main am Rhein: Philipp von Zabern, 1982), pp. 196–219.

Paul Bril 1554–1626

6

Landscape with Shepherds
Oil on copper, 12.6 x 16.6 cm

6a Infrared detail of *Landscape with Shepherds*

Bril, a native of Antwerp, traveled to Rome sometime before 1582 and remained there until his death in 1626. In Italy he began as an assistant to his elder brother, Matthijs, who was involved in painting frescoes for the Vatican. He soon received numerous commissions for both murals and easel paintings. His landscapes, which stress the picturesque aspects of nature, had a strong influence on artists working in Rome, many of whom helped to spread his influence to the North.

This small painting on copper, reproduced in its actual size, dates from Bril's late period.[1] It shows his interest in the "classical" or ideal landscape so popular among his Italian contemporaries. Through a careful orchestration of light and shadow, Bril creates a vast space and, at the same time, calls attention to the gentle contours of the land. The tall trees on either side add a majestic note, dwarfing the two shepherds in the middle distance and a third figure seated at the right.

The foreground originally included three figures, two of which were painted out. This change in composition, which is barely visible to the naked eye, can be better seen in an infrared detail (fig. 6a). One of the figures that was eliminated stands in profile just to the right of center. He wears a hat and holds a sack on his back with his right hand and extends his left arm toward the seated figure. The other, also wearing a hat, sits on a rock farther back between him and the seated figure in blue. By reducing the number of figures in the foreground, Bril gives greater emphasis to the two in the distance, whose silhouetted forms serve as a transition between the shadowy foreground and the sun-bathed hills beyond.

Provenance: Sale, Plaza Art Galleries, N.Y., ca. 1938; Coll. Mr. and Mrs. Julius S. Held.

Exhibition: *Paintings and Sculpture from the Collection of Mr. and Mrs. Julius S. Held*, Smith College Museum of Art, Northampton, Mass., 1–27 October 1968, no. 15.

---

1 The attribution to Bril was first suggested by Charles Sterling.

Jan Brueghel the Elder *1568–1625*

7

Port Scene in Venice

Oil on copper, 19.5 x 23.5 cm

7a Detail of *Port Scene in Venice*

The gondolas associate this imaginary scene with Venice, and the domed structure in the distance may refer to the island church of San Giorgio Maggiore, which was constructed during the second half of the sixteenth century. The buildings at the left combine both Netherlandish and Italian elements. While the two large vessels anchored at the right could be found in any major port, most of those around the dock are river barges from northern Europe and would never have traveled as far as Venice.[1]

Numerous, tiny figures in brightly colored costumes are scattered about the boats and dock (see Frontispiece). Like ants on an anthill, they convey the hustle and bustle of the transient environment. Conducting business, loading cargo, preparing boats, or simply relaxing between voyages, they are everywhere, even on top of one of the buildings at the left. Some wear turbans, suggesting the Middle Eastern influence on Venice, which had long been the major trading center between Europe and Asia.

The port is clearly a man's world. The only woman in the entire scene is set off in a gondola at the lower right (fig. 7a). Fashionably dressed and wearing her blonde hair in a miter headdress characteristic of northern Italy (fig. 7b), she sits next to a swarthy mustachioed man who also appears to be Italian. The couple's leisurely cruise about the harbor illustrates one of Venice's oldest traditions.

Once attributed to Abel Grimmer, this painting is now associated with Jan Brueghel the Elder. Its high quality and close connections with other works by Brueghel make the present attribution the most plausible one. The painting can be compared with *Sailboats near a Village* (fig. 7c), which is reported to bear a Brueghel signature and partially legible date of 1600.[2] In this Netherlandish scene, the focus is on a similar gathering of sailboats, which are also viewed from above.[3] Adding color to the boats and adjacent land areas are numerous small figures that are strikingly similar to those in the Venetian scene.[4] Several even take the same poses, such as the man stretched out on top of one of the barges, his arms raised over his head. In both paintings the water is rendered in a similar fashion with attention to the reflections of the various vessels. The foregrounds are characterized by rich, blue green, transparent tones that melt into a strongly lighted area in the distance.

7b Pieter van den Keere, Flemish, 1571–ca. 1646, detail from map of Italy, 1616, engraving. Bayerische Staatsbibliothek, Munich

As both Klauner and Ertz have pointed out, *Sailboats near a Village* exhibits a progressive handling of space that began to appear in Brueghel's work around 1600. It was at this time that the Flemish master departed from his panoramic views of the sixteenth century to concentrate on smaller scenes.

7c Brueghel, *Sailboats near a Village*, 1600?, copper, 25.6 x 36 cm. Formerly Coll. Koenigs, Sweden (photo: courtesy De Boer)

By abandoning framing devices and separate divisions of space, the artist gives the viewer more immediate contact with the subject. This more unified composition, which became a hallmark of seventeenth-century landscape and marine painting, is also seen in *Port Scene in Venice*. As in *Sailboats near a Village*, the slightly elevated view is a carry over from the preceding century.

The inclusion of Netherlandish barges suggests that *Port Scene in Venice* was painted in Flanders and not Italy, despite the subject.[5] Although Brueghel lived in Italy from 1590 to 1596, there is no record of his having visited Venice. The Venetian elements in the painting may well have been taken from works by other artists. Italianate figures and architecture appear in many of the paintings Brueghel made following his return to the Netherlands.[6]

Provenance: Victor Decock sale, Galerie Charpentier, Paris, 12 May 1948, no. 61, as by Abel Grimmer (illus.); Didier Aaron, Inc., N.Y., 1983; Mr. and Mrs. Robert Cushman.

1 The spritsail on several of the barges is not an Italian rigging. I am grateful to J. van Beylen, formerly of the Nationaal Scheepvaartmuseum, Antwerp, for his comments on the vessels.

2 See F. Klauner, "Zur Landschaft Jan Brueghels d. Ä.," *Nationalmusei Årsbok*, 1949–50, pp. 15–16, fig. 7, and K. Ertz, *Jan Brueghel der Ältere...* (Cologne: DuMont, 1979), pp. 184 –86, fig. 213, cat. no. 68. Like Ertz, I have not had the opportunity to see the original painting. The last digit of the date is illegible. Ertz agrees with the date 1600 that is given by Klauner.

3 The painting appears to have been the inspiration for a similar, later composition, which is one of a pair attributed to Jan Brueghel the Younger; see De Jonckheere's catalogue for *XIIe Biennale mostra mercato, internazionale dell' antiquariato*, Palazzo Strozzi, Florence, 19 September–11 October 1981, no. 11, with monogrammed pendant (illus.).

4 See the color illustration in *Modernen van toen 1570–1630: Vlaamse schilderkunst en haar invloed*, exh. cat. (Laren: Singer Museum, 1963), no. 34.

5 The leeboard that appears on one of the barges came into use around 1600.

6 A woman wearing the same style of headdress as the woman in the gondola appears in Brueghel's *Preaching of Saint John the Baptist*, which Ertz (no. 53) dates around 1598, and *Landscape with the Young Tobias* (Coll. Liechtenstein, Vaduz; Ertz, no. 47), dated 1598.

Pieter Brueghel the Younger   1564-5–1637-8

8

The Marriage Procession, 1623
Oil on panel, 68.1 x 122.7 cm

Pieter Brueghel the Younger devoted himself almost entirely to reproducing works by his father, Pieter Brueghel the Elder. No more than four or five years old when his father died in 1569, the son never actually studied with his father; and since most of the latter's paintings were dispersed by the time he began his career, Pieter the Younger undoubtedly relied on drawings and engravings for his copying.[1] The great demand for reproductions of the elder Brueghel's paintings is evidenced by the vast number in existence, including an estimated twenty-six after a single composition.[2] Judging from the numerous copies and their variation in style, the son probably had a large workshop.

The younger Brueghel painted at least eight copies of *The Marriage Procession* after a work by his father; all appear to have been done toward the end of his career.[3] What is thought to be the finest version (fig. 8a), now in the city museum in Brussels, is considered by some to be the original.[4] Stylistically, the composition dates from the end of the father's career, around 1565. The copy shown here has often been confused with another work by the son at the Musée du Petit Palais; both are signed and are the earliest dated versions (1623; fig. 8b).[5]

In this version, the subtle handling and atmospheric effects of the father's work are sacrificed for more intense color and greater simplification of form. Both the figures and landscape are rendered in a more linear, mechanical fashion, with the "outlined" quality of the figures detracting from the overall unity of the group. A comparison with the Brussels painting suggests that the son also took some liberties with the composition and eliminated several elements, including a shepherd and an animal skull in the right foreground (fig. 8a).

Brueghel's colorful tableau shows a typical Flemish wedding procession as it makes its way along a road toward the church at the upper left. According to custom, the men and women walk separately. The groom appears at the left, framed by two trees and wearing the traditional wedding crown atop his bright red cap. The other men follow, led by two who are probably the fathers of the bridal couple. The bride, rather plump and solemn and flanked by a pair of equally solemn youths, is followed by two women who are probably

8a Pieter Brueghel the Elder, Flemish, 1525-30–1569, *The Wedding Procession,* panel, 61.5 x 114.5 cm. Musée Communal, Brussels (photo: A.C.L., Brussels)

8b Pieter Brueghel the Younger, *The Wedding Procession,* 1623, panel, 73 x 123.5 cm. Musée du Petit Palais, Paris

the mothers. In contrast to the other women in the procession, the bride wears her hair down and uncovered except for the wedding crown.[6] The bride and the groom are each preceded by a man playing the bagpipe, the traditional instrument at Flemish weddings and kermises. The type of instrument shown here – with two drones, one slightly longer than the other – is known as the "Brueghel bagpipe" because of its frequent appearance in pictures by the elder Brueghel.[7]

8c Detail from *The Marriage Procession*

The vast fields that stretch into the background are devoid of working peasants, suggesting a holiday. Although sacks of grain are seen next to the windmill, there are no laborers here either. The only activity occurs in the village at the right, where preparations are being made for the wedding feast that will soon take place (fig. 8c).

The festivities and rituals connected with peasant weddings are the subject of two other paintings by Pieter Brueghel the Elder;[8] Pieter the Younger also painted two original compositions of the theme.[9] The elder Brueghel would often disguise himself as a peasant and join the rural folk at weddings and fairs in order to observe their character and activities as preparation for his paintings.[10] In *The Marriage Procession,* he shows his ability to capture the personalities of a variety of people, both young and old—not to mention a dog, whose reaction to the sound of the bagpipe did not go unnoticed. The composition is a visual encyclopedia of one of the most important days in a peasant's life—an image that would have charmed both lower and upper class alike. It is no wonder that his son reproduced it so often.

Signed and dated lower right ·*P·BREVGHEL· 1623·*

Verso: From former frame, label from 1935 Orangerie exhibition; two labels from 1936 Rijksmuseum exhibition, one inscribed *Bacri/819;* two labels from the Paris packer Ch. Pottier, one inscribed…*M Bacri,* the other stamped *261;* a label from the French packer J. Chenue inscribed *A S R New York;* a small, circular label inscribed *1009.*

Provenance: Count Léon Mniszech, Paris; sale, Galerie Georges Petit, Paris, 9–11 April 1902, no. 97 (*La Promenade;* illus.); MM. Bacri, Paris; Arnold, Seligmann Rey & Co., N.Y., 1938; Aldus C. Higgins, Worcester, Mass.; Mr. and Mrs. Milton P. Higgins.

References: R. van Bastelaer and G. H. de Loo, *Peter Brueghel l'Ancien: Son oeuvre et son temps* (Brussels: G. van Oest, 1907), p. 354; E. Michel, *Brueghel* (Paris: Les Editions G. Cres, 1931), p. 83; G. Glück, *Das grosse Bruegel-Werk* (Vienna: Anton Schroll & Co., 1932), p. 67; G. Glück, *Bruegels Gemälde* (Vienna: Anton Schroll & Co., 1932), p. 99, no. 71; *Worcester Art Museum News Bulletin and Calendar* 16, no. 2 (November 1950): 9 (illus.); G. Marlier, *Pierre Brueghel le Jeune: Edition posthume mise au point et annotée par Jacqueline Folie* (Brussels: Robert Finck, 1969), p. 172, no. 2, fig. 94 (see n. 5).

Exhibitions: *De Van Eyck à Bruegel,* Musée de l'Orangerie, Paris, 1935, no. 19; *Tentoonstelling van oude kunst uit het bezit van den internationalen handel,* Rijksmuseum, July – September 1936, no. 21; *The Worcester-Philadelphia Exhibition of Flemish Painting,* Worcester Art Museum, 23 February – 12 March 1939, J. G. Johnson Collection at the Philadelphia Museum of Art, 25 March – 26 April 1939, no. 112; Exhibition of art objects owned in and near Worcester, Worcester Art Museum, 17 November 1950 – 1 January 1951.

---

1 The reversed images of many of his paintings suggest his dependency on engravings. See F. van Hauwaert, "La Copie chez Pierre Brueghel le Jeune," *Revue des archéologues et historiens d'art de Louvain* 11 (1978): 84–100.

2 Marlier lists twenty-six copies of *The Sermon of Saint John the Baptist,* the original of which is in the Museum of Fine Arts, Budapest (*Brueghel,* pp. 47–58). Nine of the copies are signed by Pieter the Younger and one by his elder brother, Jan.

3 In addition to this painting (1623), four others are dated: 1623, 1627, and two 1630. In his discussion of this composition, G. Marlier lists ten copies after the original, which he considers to be the work in the Musée Communal de Bruxelles (*Brueghel,* pp. 169–76; see n.2). Marlier notes that his list may mention the same work twice. Confusion between the various versions results from their strong similarities and the fact that several have exchanged hands many times during this century. This author knows of six versions besides the one exhibited here and the one in Brussels: 1) Musée Calvet, Avignon, no. 503, canvas, 150 x 284 cm (Marlier 1); 2) Musée du Petit Palais, Paris, panel, 67 x 121 cm, signed and dated 1623 (Marlier 2; see n. 5); 3) Sotheby's, N.Y., 20 January 1983, no. 66 (illus.), panel, 75 x 120.5 cm, signed and dated 1627, formerly A. and M. Carrier, Lyon (Marlier 4); 4) Sotheby's, London, 23 June 1982, no. 38 (illus.), panel, 74 x 124 cm, signed and dated 1630 (Marlier 7), formerly Coll. Boissevain, Florence, and before that Coll. Mrs. Geoffrey Hart, Brighton (Marlier 6 and 7); 5) Musée Royal des Beaux-Arts, Antwerp, no. 807, panel, 69.5 x 115.8 cm, signed and dated 1630 (Marlier 9); 6) Christie's, London, 2 December 1977, no. 78 (illus.), panel, 142 x 280 cm, formerly La Duchesse de Beaufort-Spontin (Marlier 10). In addition to these, Marlier lists two other works that were in sales of 1903 and 1914 (Marlier 5 and 8) and which may well be identical with one of the above.

There also exists an abbreviated version of the *Wedding Procession* attributed to Pieter Brueghel the Younger (Marlier, *Brueghel,* p. 176, fig. 98), as well as a drawing that is a rather free interpretation of the painted versions (Musée des Beaux-Arts, Lyon). The composition's popularity during the 17th-century is also suggested by Rubens's drawing of one of the processional figures, which is thought to have been made shortly after his return from Italy around 1609–10; see M. Jaffé, "Rubens as a Collector of Drawings, Part Three," *Master Drawings* 4, no. 2 (1966): 134, pl. 9b.

4 Formerly in the Northwick Park Collection, this work (panel, 68.5 x 114 cm) entered the Brussels museum in 1966. For references to this work, see *Pieter Brueghel l'Ancien: "Le Cortège de noces"* (Brussels: Robert Finck Galerie, 1966). For a discussion of the attribution, see W. Vanbeselaere, "Pieter Bruegel, de Oude? De bruiloftsstoet," *Openbaar kunstbezit in Vlaanderen 7*, no. 13 (1969): 13 a, b.

This painting has also been attributed to the elder Brueghel's other, more famous son, Jan. See C. de Tolnay, *Pierre Bruegel l'Ancien* (Brussels: Nouvelle Société d'éditions, 1935), p. 95; and F. Grossmann, "Flemish Paintings at Bruges," *Burlington Magazine* 99 (January 1957): 5.

5 Marlier confused the Worcester and Paris pictures (*Brueghel*, p. 172, no. 2). The major difference is the treatment of the sky: in the Paris picture it is lighter and has soft, gray clouds instead of the intense blue clouds of this painting. The provenance of the Paris work is correctly given here for the first time: Coll. Renz, Munich; sale, Helbing, Munich, 18/19 December 1917, no. 571 (illus.); Chillingworth sale, Galeries Fischer, Lucerne, 5 September 1922, no. 14 (illus.); part of Don Charles Vincent Ocampo estate placed at the Musée du Petit Palais in 1930; acquired by museum in 1945. I am grateful to Gilles Chazal of the Musée du Petit Palais for assisting me in reconstructing the provenance.

6 The tradition of long hair and a bridal crown is discussed by W.S. Gibson, "Some Notes on Pieter Bruegel the Elder's *Peasant Wedding Feast*," *Art Quarterly* 28 (1965): 197, 203, n.19.

7 See R.D. Leppert, *The Theme of Music in Flemish Paintings of the Seventeenth Century*, 2 vols. (Munich-Salzburg: Musikverlag Emil Katzbichler, 1977), 1:178–79.

8 The elder Brueghel's two other wedding pictures were also painted late in his career: *The Wedding Dance in Open Air*, 1566 (Detroit) and *Peasant Wedding Feast*, ca. 1657 (Vienna).

9 One shows the groom followed by the men, the other the bride followed by the women. Several versions of this set are known. For illustrations of two, see E. Scheyer, "*The Wedding Dance* by Pieter Bruegel the Elder in the Detroit Institute of Arts: Its Relations and Derivations," *Art Quarterly* 28, no. 3 (1965): 180–81, figs. 6–9.

10 See K. van Mander, *Het schilder-boeck...* (Haarlem: Paschier van Wesbusch, 1604), p. 223.

Hendrik van Cleve III *1525–1589*

9

The Building of the Tower of Babel
Oil on panel, 60.5 x 71.5 cm

The Tower of Babel has long been a favorite subject of artists. It was already a common motif in the Middle Ages, appearing often in illuminations, frescoes, and mosaics. By the sixteenth century, it had become a standard theme among painters and printmakers,[1] and was especially popular among Flemish artists like Van Cleve who were interested in antique architecture, which they studied in Italy.[2]

According to the Old Testament (Genesis 11:1-9), after the Great Flood, the descendants of Noah set out to build on a plain in the land of Shinar "a city and a tower with its top in the heavens." To suggest the Near East, Van Cleve adds a crescent, symbol of the Turkish Empire, to several buildings, but he departs from the biblical account by placing the tower in a hilly land near the sea. He also shows the tower being constructed of stone and mortar instead of brick and bitumen, as described in the Bible.

In the foreground, masons measure and cut stone, while workmen behind haul sacks of limestone to two kilns at the right. The elderly figure accompanied by an assistant at the lower right may be a supervisor, and the man in a turban at the far left may be Nimrod, the legendary conqueror of Babylon who reputedly oversaw the construction. In the background, countless ant-sized figures convey a sense of great activity and scale.

Van Cleve did several versions of the Tower of Babel. His painting in the Hamburg Museum (fig. 9a), for example, shows his characteristic rounded tower and long entrance ramp, and its landscape and buildings are painted in the same earth tones set against a brilliant turquoise sky. Another version by Van Cleve is even closer to the work exhibited here in terms of the architectural elements and their arrangement (fig. 9b).[3]

9a Van Cleve, *Tower of Babel*, panel, 40.5 x 55 cm. Kunsthalle, Hamburg

9b Van Cleve, *Tower of Babel*, panel, 45 x 65 cm. Present whereabouts unknown (photo: Marburg)

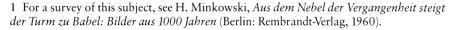

Provenance: Dealer, C.P.A. & G.R. Castendijk, Rotterdam; sale, Mak van Waay, Amsterdam, 10 May 1971, no. 38 (illus.); sale, Palais des Beaux-Arts, Brussels, 26 October 1971; Kunsthandel P. de Boer, Amsterdam, 1972, no. 6 (illus.); private collection.

1 For a survey of this subject, see H. Minkowski, *Aus dem Nebel der Vergangenheit steigt der Turm zu Babel: Bilder aus 1000 Jahren* (Berlin: Rembrandt-Verlag, 1960).

2 See V. Terlinden, "Une vue de Rome, par Hendrik van Cleve," *Bulletin Musées Royaux des Beaux-Arts, Bruxelles* 26 (1961): 165–74.

3 This painting was last recorded in the Mossel sale at Frederik Muller & Co., Amsterdam, 11–18 March 1954, no. 668. In Minkowski's *Aus dem Nebel*, it is reversed (fig. 170).

Jan Cossiers 1600–1671

10

Portrait of a Man
Oil on panel, 62.2 x 48.3 cm

Jan Cossiers, an Antwerp artist who trained first with his father and then with Cornelis de Vos (see cat. no. 37), lived from 1623 to 1626 in Aix-en-Provence, where he was influenced by followers of Caravaggio. He was back in Antwerp by 1628, the year he joined the painters' guild. During the following decade, he assisted Rubens with two major painting commissions.[1]

This portrait, which appears to date from the 1630s, shows the marked chiaroscuro of the Caravaggio tradition. The dramatic lighting, warm palette, and rich display of brushwork are all key factors in giving a sense of immediacy to the subject. From thin, transparent shadows to thick, juicy highlights, Cossiers maintains a fresh and lively application of paint throughout. As in the best of Baroque portraits, his bold brushwork does not preclude attention to detail: a few short, quick strokes, for example, capture not only the folds under the man's chin, but the stubble of beard on it as well. These and other carefully observed features like the blood-shot eyes, red nose, and slightly knitted brow give insight into the character of the smugly posed sitter.[2]

Cossiers's portrait skills are also demonstrated in chalk drawings that rank among the finest of the period and exhibit the same spontaneous execution. The high quality of his portraits has resulted in the misattribution of many works to some of his better-known contemporaries, including this painting, which was formerly given to Jacob Jordaens.[3]

Provenance: Devonshire Collection, Chatsworth, as by Jacob Jordaens, cat. no. 305; sale, Christie's, London, 31 October 1975, no. 74, as by Jordaens; Hoogsteder-Naumann, Ltd., N.Y., 1983; private collection.

1 The decorations for the triumphal entry into Antwerp of Cardinal-Infante Ferdinand (1635) and the series of paintings for the Torre de la Parada near Madrid (1637). See M.-L. Hairs, *Dans le sillage de Rubens: Les Peintres d'histoire anversois au XVIIᵉ siècle* (Liège: Université de Liège, 1977), pp. 31–32.

2 Cossiers used a very similar pose for his own self-portrait, an engraving of which appears in Cornelis de Bie, *Het gulden cabinet...* (Antwerp: J. Meyssens, 1661), p. 267.

3 Another example is Cossiers's *Portrait of a Gentleman* in the Detroit Institute of Arts, which, until recent discovery of a signature, was attributed to Anthony van Dyck. See J.S. Held, *Flemish and German Paintings of the 17th Century* (Detroit: Detroit Institute of Arts, 1982), pp. 25–26, pl. 2.

Jacques Foucquier   1590–1659

11

Landscape
Oil on panel, 57.7 x 84.7 cm[1]

This landscape, formerly thought to be by the Brussels artist Jacques d'Arthois, is here attributed to Jacques Foucquier.[2] An Antwerp mark on the back supports the new attribution to Foucquier, who began his career in that city (fig. 11a). Branded in the wood and consisting of a three-towered citadel beneath a pair of hands, it indicates that the panel was approved by the Antwerp painters' guild.[3]

Foucquier, who is thought to have been born in Antwerp,[4] was registered there as a master in the painters' guild in 1614. By 1616 he was a member of the Brussels guild, and soon afterwards he was at Heidelberg in the service of the Elector of the Palatinate. According to Félibien, he moved to Paris in 1621; there he collaborated with Rubens. By 1626 Foucquier was at Toulon, employed by Louis XIII to make paintings for the Louvre, a project in which he later competed with Poussin.

In contrast to his drawings, examples of which are preserved from throughout his career, Foucquier's paintings are rather rare. Most of his large works, which were painted later in his career, have disappeared, leaving only a small number of pictures from before 1623, several of which, like this one, have only recently been recognized as his work.[5] All of this may explain why Foucquier is so little known today, though in the eighteenth century he was considered among the most important landscape artists.

This painting should be compared with Foucquier's *View of a River Valley,* signed and dated 1617 (fig. 11b). Both landscapes show a characteristic broad handling that reflects the influence of Joos de Momper, with whom Foucquier is recorded to have studied. The briskly painted figures in the foregound, which serve as the focal point of both pictures, suggest the influence of another Antwerp artist, Jan Brueghel the Elder. Here they add a vibrant note to an already colorful landscape. Less detailed, but equally picturesque, are the horse-drawn covered wagon silhouetted against the horizon and the shepherd and his flock moving along the water's edge at the lower right.

Like *View of a River Valley,* this painting features a centrally placed oak tree with a view into the distance on either side.[6] In both works the road on the left serves as a transition between the foreground and background, which here includes a beautiful progression of green and blue tones. The strong connections between the two works suggest they were painted about the same time.[7] Both paintings demonstrate Foucquier's importance as a link between the De Momper landscape tradition of Antwerp and the school of decorative

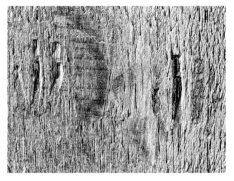

11a Brand of Antwerp

11b Foucquier, *View of a River Valley,* 1617, panel, 33 x 43.2 cm. Present whereabouts unknown

landscape painting that developed in Brussels shortly after Foucquier's stay there. After his move to France, Foucquier himself turned more and more to a classical style under the influence of artists like Paul Bril (see cat. no. 6).

Verso: Brand of Antwerp including two hands, partly visible (dimensions of citadel mark: 2.1 x 2.7 cm).

Provenance: Brod Gallery, London; private collection.

1 This measurement includes a strip 2.8 centimeters wide that was later added at the top of the painting and is now concealed by the frame.

2 The two most important studies on Foucquier are by Wolfgang Stechow: "Jacques Foucquier," *De Kunst der Nederlanden* 1 (February 1931): 297–303; "Drawings and Etchings by Jacques Foucquier," *Gazette des Beaux-Arts* 34 (1948): 419–34.

3 The hand symbol (more legible on the back of cat. nos. 19 and 35) derives from the name of the city, which according to the most popular legend, comes from *hand werpen* ("to throw the hand"), a reference to the mythological Roman giant, Druon Antigonus, who cut off the hands of mariners who sailed past his castle without paying tolls and then threw the hands in the Schelt.

Little has been written on panel marks outside of G. Gepts's article, "Tafereelmaker Michiel Vriendt, leverancier van Rubens," *Jaarboek Koninklijk Museum voor Schone Kunsten, Antwerpen,* 1954–60, pp. 83–87.

4 See P.-E. Claessens, "Deux points à éclaircir dans la vie du peintre flamand Jacques Foucquier (ca. 1590–1659)," *L'Intermédiaire des genéalogistes,* November 1965, pp. 305–7.

5 See, for example, I. Ember, "Un Paysage de Jacques Foucquier au Musée des Beaux Arts," *Bulletin du Musée Hongrois des Beaux-Arts,* no. 50 (1978): 63–72.

6 This compositional motif appears in several of Foucquier's works from the same period. See, for example, his *Winter Landscape* at the Fitzwilliam Museum, Cambridge (1617), and the tondo landscape at the Musée des Beaux-Arts, Ghent.

7 Given the Antwerp mark on this panel, it is likely that the work was painted in Antwerp before he moved to Brussels.

Frans Francken the Younger *1581–1642*

12

Lamentation
Oil on panel, 33.5 x 48.5 cm

Frans Francken the Younger was the most productive and well-known member of a family of Antwerp artists that spanned almost two centuries. He painted a variety of subjects, almost all on a small scale, and like his son, he often added figures to paintings by other artists, as in the landscape by Govaerts (cat. no. 15).

Francken painted many scenes from the Passion of Christ. In this depiction of the Lamentation, a theme that dates from the late Middle Ages, he shows Christ just after he was taken down from the cross.[1] The grief-stricken Virgin kneels by her dead son, surrounded by Saint John the Evangelist, Mary Magdalen, and an older woman. The man at the left, wearing a turban and a halo and supporting the body of Christ, is Joseph of Arimathaea, who received permission from Pontius Pilate to take the body and place it in his own tomb. Nicodemus, a Pharisee who assisted with the burial, stands at the right holding the crown of thorns. Behind him a youth prepares the tomb.

The blood-stained sponge and nails in the left foreground recall the crucifixion, as do the crosses on the distant hill. The decorative jar at the right may belong to the Magdalen, who annointed the feet of Christ, or to Nicodemus, who brought a mixture of myrrh and aloes to preserve the body.

Francken painted several other Lamentations, including a vertical composition with essentially the same group of figures (fig. 12a). In both paintings, his ability as a figure painter is especially evident in the rendering of Christ. Stretched across the picture plane and outlined by a white sheet, the lifeless and bloodied body forces the viewer to contemplate the horrors of the Passion. This type of devotional image was particularly popular during the Counter Reformation, when religious art was used as an emotional stimulus to piety. The somber mood, however, is offset by the painting's intense colors and rich surfaces. The artist even incorporated metallic gold, which is more often associated with medieval painting. The gold, reduced to a powder and combined with the oil medium, appears in the four halos, the collar of Nicodemus's robe, and the turban and cloak of Joseph of Arimathaea.

f ffrancken in et f!

12a Francken the Younger, *Lamentation of Christ*, copper, 35 x 28.5 cm. Galerie Fischer, Lucerne

The colorful palette and somewhat crowded composition suggest that the *Lamentation* was painted in the mid-1620s. It was at this time, when his father was no longer living, that Francken stopped referring to himself as the younger. After his own son, Frans III, began painting around 1628, he often added "the elder" to his signature.

12b Panel mark of Lambrecht Steens

The back of Francken's painting includes a monogram punched into the wood (fig. 12b). This mark, consisting of the letters *L* and *S,* appears to be that of Lambrecht Steens, a panel maker who became a master in the Antwerp guild in 1608.[2] The same monogram appears on many other panels from this period, often with the mark of the Antwerp guild, as in two Rubens modelli from 1620.[3]

Signed lower right *f francken in et f(.)*

Verso: Panel maker's mark *LS* (1.8 x .9 cm); in black paint the number *XXXVI;* seal in red wax with a coat of arms containing the monogram *TB* or *FB* surmounted by a crown.

Provenance: American private collection; Paul Drey Gallery, N.Y., 1968; private collection.

---

1 Two variants of this painting are recorded. One sold by J.A. de Waart & Zonen (The Hague, 30 May–1 June 1967, no. 41, panel, 36 x 49 cm; illus.) is virtually the same composition, with the exception of the position of Saint John's hands and the addition of two figures in front of the crosses on the hill. The other painting, sold by C.J. Wawra (Vienna, 16 April 1923, no. 243, panel, 40 x 59 cm; illus.), has the same variations as the painting sold by De Waart; however, the composition extends more to the right and includes an additional youth preparing the sepulcher. The possibility that the painting shown here might also have included a second youth, who was eliminated when the panel was trimmed, is ruled out by the fact that the panel, which is beveled on all sides, includes original paint on the right edge.

2 Steens's name appears quite often in the guild records between 1608 and 1651. See P. Rombouts and T. van Lerius, *Les Liggeren et autres archives historiques de la Gilde Anversoise de Saint Luc,* 2 vols. (Antwerp: Baggerman, 1864–75), 1: 446, 452, 544, 577; 2: 117, 122, 220.

3 See J. S. Held, *The Oil Sketches of Peter Paul Rubens: A Critical Catalogue,* 2 vols. (Princeton: Princeton University Press, 1980), nos. 27, 36.

Jan Fyt *1611–1661*

13

Still Life with a Dog
Oil on canvas, 87 x 117 cm

Jan Fyt, a specialist in the painting of game, was the leading pupil of the great animal painter Frans Snyders. In his day, Fyt's pictures of dead game were considered trophies of the hunt and were produced in great number. And it was Fyt who popularized the practice of incorporating this type of still life into a landscape.[1]

In this painting, the natural, evening setting serves as a foil to the dramatically lighted arrangement in the foreground.[2] Adding to the theatrical effect is the red drape pulled across the column at the upper right. The game—a hare and two partridges—shares the spotlight with a large, green squash and a basket of fruit, which includes some figs inside a Chinese porcelain bowl. To counterbalance the colorful display at the left, Fyt has arranged the dead animals so that the most variegated parts of their bodies are shown. The extremely tactile quality he imparts to the fur and plumage adds to the animals' presence.

The small, brown-and-white dog that peeks out from behind the column calls attention to the hunting theme, which is also implied by the looped branch in front of him, a device used for stringing up small birds. Although once a very common species used specifically for hunting partridge, the dog no longer exists as a purebred.

Signed at right, on stone base *Joannes·Fyt·*

Verso: Viennese export label and label inscribed *...voll signirt/Johannes Fyt;* label on frame *DR. LILIENFELD.*

Provenance: Charles Brunner Galerie, Paris, 1914, no. 21 (illus.); Dr. Leon Lilienfeld, Vienna; sale, Sotheby Parke-Bernet, N.Y., 17–18 May 1972, no. 28 (illus.); H. Shickman Gallery, N.Y., 1980; private collection.

Reference: G. Glück, *Niederländische Gemälde aus der Sammlung des Herrn Dr. Leon Lilienfeld in Wien* (Vienna: Verlag der Gesellschaft für Vervielfältigende Kunst, 1917), pp. 12, 62, no. 20, illus.

---

1 See S.A. Sullivan, "The Dutch Game Piece" (Ph.D. diss., Case Western Reserve University, 1978), p. 59.

2 A copy after this painting, which does not include the landscape at the left or dog at the right, is in the Johnson Collection, Philadelphia Museum of Art, no. 703.

Joannes·Fyt·

Jan Gossaert (Mabuse) *ca. 1478–1532*

14

Mary Magdalen
Oil on cradled panel, 51.3 x 39.6 cm

Jan Gossaert, whose other name, Mabuse, derives from his hometown of Maubeuge in Hainaut, may have studied in Bruges before joining the Antwerp guild in 1503. In 1508 he went to Italy for a year with his patron, Philip of Burgundy, in order to record the art of the antique. His interest in ancient Rome and the Renaissance was a key factor in introducing the classical tradition into Flemish art.

Although rather stylized, Gossaert's *Magdalen* may be a portrait, for it was not uncommon for someone to be painted in the guise of a religious figure, particularly one's patron saint.[1] At this time, it was also popular to show the Magdalen before her conversion, wearing rich attire and covered with jewels. Such opulent dress was favored by the court and upper class. Later, during the Baroque period, the Magdalen was more often depicted as a penitent, renouncing worldly pleasures.

The saint's fashionable costume features embroidered, slashed sleeves that form a framework for puffs of white sleeve pulled out from underneath. Equally elaborate is the upper part of her bodice, a diaphanous material decorated with fine gold needlework and rows of pearls. Pearls also adorn the saint's long, golden red hair, and draped across her shoulders is an ornate chain containing precious stones that repeat the colors of her dress. Gossaert has taken every opportunity to embellish his subject; even her hands are arranged so that the fingers form a decorative design.

The Magdalen's regal attire complements her imperious bearing. Looking toward the viewer out of the corner of her eye, she also has a rather coy appearance. A pentimento shows that the saint's left eye was originally larger, but the artist reduced it slightly to create a more seductive look.[2]

Gossaert has depicted the Magdalen holding her most common attribute, the jar of ointment with which she annointed Christ's feet. Unusually large, the container is also an excuse for the artist to show his interest in the antique: the bronze urn is decorated with classical details, including acanthus leaves and an elaborate relief of rams' heads and swags.

In this well-preserved panel—which is thought to have been painted late in Gossaert's career, when he lived mainly at Middleburg[3]—one can fully appreciate the artist's craftsmanship, in particular the inimitable, enamel-like surfaces that made him a favorite among royal patrons of the day. There is another version of this painting in the Museum Mayer van den Bergh,

14a After Gossaert, *Magdalen*, panel, 51.5
x 39.8 cm. Museum Mayer van den Bergh,
Antwerp (photo: A.C.L., Brussels)

Antwerp (fig. 14a), which was once thought to be the original, but is now
considered a copy or studio work. The superiority of the painting shown here
was demonstrated in 1965, when the two works were exhibited together for
the first time.[4] Missing in the Antwerp painting is Gossaert's delicate modeling, particularly in the drapery and decorative urn, and the luminous surfaces

that are found throughout this work, even in the shadows.[5] The numerous versions of Gossaert's late paintings suggest that toward the end of his career he had a large workshop.[6] None of his followers, however, ever succeeded in duplicating his refined technique.

Verso: On frame, loan labels from Busch-Reisinger Museum (no. 51.1967) and Museum of Fine Arts, Boston (no. TL 12, 930; Oct. 5, 1965).

Provenance: Sale, Drouot, Paris, 14 March 1918, no. 3 *(Portrait de femme),* as by Bernaert van Orley (illus.); Coll. Claude Lafontaine, Paris; sale, Palais Galliera, Paris, 10 April 1962, no. 8 *(Portrait de jeune femme;* illus.); dealer, Rosenberg & Stiebel, N.Y.; William A. Coolidge.

References: H. Pauwels, H.R. Hoetink, and S. Herzog, *Jean Gossaert dit Mabuse,* exh. cat. (Rotterdam: Museum Boymans-van Beuningen, 1965), p. 204, 207, no. 35 (illus.); H. Börsch-Supan, "Zu der Ausstellung Gossaert," *Kunstchronik* 18 (1965): 201; S. Herzog, "Jan Gossart Called Mabuse (ca. 1478–1532): A Study of His Chronology with a Catalogue of His Works" (Ph.D. diss., Bryn Mawr College, 1968), pp. 155–56, 302–3, no. 47, pl. 56; J. Rasmussen, "Zum Meister H. L.," *Jahrbuch der Hamburger Kunstsammlungen* 18 (1973): 63, n. 18; J. de Coo, *Museum Mayer van den Bergh* (Antwerp: Govaerts, 1978), pp. 70–71.

Exhibitions: *Jean Gossaert dit Mabuse,* Museum Boymans-van Beuningen, Rotterdam, 15 May–27 June 1965 and Groeningemuseum, Bruges, 10 July–31 August 1965; *Northern Renaissance Art,* Busch-Reisinger Museum, Cambridge, Mass., 13 February–1 April 1967.

---

1 See, for example, the portrait of Isabella of Austria that is sometimes attributed to Gossaert (Musées Royaux des Beaux-Arts de Belgique, Brussels, no. 4341), reproduced in *Le Siècle de Bruegel,* exh. cat. (Brussels: Musées Royaux des Beaux-Arts de Belgique, 1963), no. 117, fig. 78.

2 Several other small pentimenti appear along the hands, the side of the face, and her left shoulder. These subtle changes indicate the calculating manner in which Gossaert worked.

3 A date after 1525 is suggested by both the costume and the way in which the figure is placed in an interior setting, a format Gossaert used in other late works.

4 See Börsch-Supan, "Ausstellung Gossaert," p. 201. Another Magdalen now considered to be by a follower of Gossaert is in the National Gallery, London (no. 2163).

5 The only variations between the Coolidge and the Mayer van den Bergh paintings occur in the lower part of the left sleeve. In the latter, the embroidered design is slightly different and two of the narrow bands are missing.

6 See Herzog, "Gossart," pp. 155ff.

Abraham Govaerts *1589–1626*
Frans Francken the Younger *1581–1642*

15

Landscape with Diana and Her Nymphs
Oil on copper, supported by cradle, 32 x 40.8 cm

Like so many of Govaerts's unsigned landscapes, this work was formerly attributed to Jan Brueghel the Elder.[1] Although influenced by Brueghel, Govaerts was more affected by the forest scenes of Gillis van Coninxloo, one of the major contributors to this genre.[2] In this landscape, the mythological figures were added by Frans Francken the Younger, one of Antwerp's most prolific painters (see cat. no. 12). Govaerts often collaborated with other artists, but in some cases, particularly genre scenes, he painted the figures himself.[3]

Diana, goddess of the forest and the hunt, was a favorite subject of Govaerts and an appropriate accompaniment to his lush woodland interiors.[4] Dressed in blue and yellow and wearing a small crescent on her head, she sits beneath a large oak tree with two of her nymphs and a pair of dogs. Next to her is a hunting horn and behind her some spears. The two women in the middle distance, judging from the spear held by one and the accompanying dogs, are also Diana's companions. Farther back, to the right, two men and some dogs are running through the woods—a chase scene that may refer to hunting in general, rather than a specific story.[5]

Picturesque details like broken branches and colorful flowers are common in Govaerts's imaginary scenes. All of the blossoms to the right of Diana are invented. The only flowers that can be identified are the yellow or water flag *(Iris pseudacorus)* at the far left, Flanders's only native iris, and the purple or flag iris *(Iris germanica)* in the center—which is not a water plant, as Govaerts suggests.

There has been little study of the chronology of Govaerts's work, but a comparison of some of his dated paintings suggests that this one represents his late style. *Apollo and the Nine Muses* from 1613 (fig. 15a), for example, exhibits a more complex landscape with numerous vistas that invite the viewer to explore a variety of terrains. By contrast, Govaerts's *Rape of Europa* of 1621 is a more unified landscape with less attention paid to the background (fig. 15b). As in the painting exhibited here, the artist concentrates on a few selected foreground elements like the flowers and some branches on the large oak at the right.[6]

A close examination of *Landscape with Diana and Her Nymphs* indicates that originally it probably included additional figurative elements just to the left of Diana and her companions. One can barely make out, for example, the head and forelegs of another dog. There also may have been another figure, which would help to explain the gesture of the woman next to Diana. Perhaps

15a Govaerts and Francken, *Apollo and the Nine Muses,* 1613, panel, 69 x 110.5 cm. Private collection

15b Govaerts and Francken, *Rape of Europa,* 1621, panel, 52 x 75 cm. Koninklijk Museum Schone Kunsten, Antwerp

the painting represented a specific mythological event, such as Diana's confrontation with the hunter Actaeon or the nymph Callisto. Ordinarily an X-ray might help reveal such changes in design; in this case, however, such photography is ineffective because of the painting's copper support.

Verso: Between the copper panel and the cradle, a paper with printed French text.

Provenance: Private collection, Boston; Nordest Gallery, Boston; Coll. Maida and George Abrams.

1 A cartouche at the top of the painting's frame bears the name Bril, so it also may have once been attributed to Paul Bril.

2 See G.S. Keyes's comments in "Landscape Drawings by Alexander Keirincx and Abraham Govaerts," *Master Drawings* 16, no. 3 (1978): 300.

3 See, for example, Y. Thiery, "'L'Auberge' d'Abraham Govaerts," *Bulletin Musées Royaux des Beaux-Arts, Bruxelles* 4 (1952): 135–38.

4 Other examples include *Diana and Callisto,* ca. 1605, panel, 45 x 61 cm, private collection; *Landscape with Resting Diana,* 1614, panel, 73 x 113 cm, Musée des Beaux-Arts, Bordeaux; *Diana and Actaeon,* panel, 59 x 92 cm, Pushkin State Museum of Fine Arts, Moscow. For a discussion and the dating of *Diana and Callisto* as well as an illustration of the Bordeaux painting, see G.L.M. Daniëls, "In de vallei van Arcadië...Diana bespied door Abraham Govaerts," *Antiek* 13, no. 9 (1978–79): 601–9.

5 Diana and Actaeon is the subject of Govaerts's painting in Moscow (see n. 4 above), the background of which includes a chase scene similar to the one in the painting exhibited here.

6 In all three of these paintings, the figures are by Francken, an artist with whom Govaerts collaborated throughout his career.

Abel Grimmer *ca. 1570–before 1619*

16

Interior of a Church
Oil on cradled panel, 34 x 39.6 cm

16a Detail of *Interior of a Church*

Like his father and teacher, Jacob, Abel Grimmer is best known for his land-scapes. Church and domestic interiors were a secondary theme in his work, but recur throughout most of his career.[1]

This view of the nave of a Gothic church seems to date from around 1600.[2] As with many early Flemish paintings of interiors, the architecture appears to be the artist's own invention. In creating the imaginary space, Grimmer used a strict perspective with a vanishing point at the main altar, partly visible behind the choir screen. A variety of other paintings, most of them triptychs, are spread throughout the church; they illustrate some of the major events in the life of Christ, from the Nativity in the right foreground to a Pietà at the entrance to the choir. One of the altarpieces, in the side chapel at the left, depicts the Baptism of Christ, an appropriate accompaniment to the baptism taking place at the far end of the nave. Grimmer's attention to detail is evident not only in the paintings, but also in objects like the poor box at the lower right, which is accompanied by a pointing hand and the instructions "place your offerings for the poor here" (fig. 16a).

Grimmer's painting shows the diversity of people and activities that one could expect to find in a church at this time. All levels of society are repre-sented, as we see in the foreground group, which includes, from left to right, a scholar or preacher, an upper-class couple, and a peasant or gypsy woman and her two children. This cross-section of society, not to mention the animals, suggests the ambiance of a town square rather than a sacred setting.

The slightly manneristic figures and animals can be attributed to Grimmer; several are repeated in other works by him.[3] Grimmer was not, however, always responsible for the staffage in his interiors. In what is perhaps his most ambitious church scene, a painting of 1595 (fig. 16b), the figures and animals are clearly by another hand.[4] Such collaboration between architectural and figure painters was quite common during this period, as we see in the Neeffs church interior (cat. no. 25).

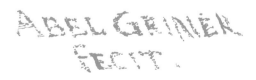

16b Grimmer, *Antwerp Cathedral*, 1595, panel, 42.2 x 57.8 cm. Present whereabouts unknown (photo: courtesy Noortman & Brod)

This view is from a much higher elevation than in the 1595 painting. As a result, the gray-and-white pattern of the tile floor becomes a major part of the composition. The floor's strict geometric design is broken up by an irregular pattern of gravestones. At the lower right, the artist has playfully incorporated his signature as an inscription on one of them.[5]

Signed on floor lower right, upside down, *ABEL GRIMER/FECIT.*

Provenance: Sale, Sotheby's, London, 10 July 1974, no. 103 (illus.); purchased by Baile; sale, Sotheby Parke Bernet, N.Y., 11 June 1981, no. 3 (illus.); private collection.

1 See F. C. Legrand, "Abel Grimmer, peintre d'architectures," *Revue belge d'archéologie et d'histoire de l'art* 26, no. 3–4 (1957): 163–67.

Grimmer's signed and dated church interiors include works from the following years: 1586 (Christie's, London, 18 April 1980, no. 65); 1588 (Kraus, Paris, September, 1976, no. 29); 1595 (formerly Chesham Coll.; fig. 16b); 1604 (Sotheby's, London, 9 March 1983, no. 3); 1606 (Galerie Charpentier, Paris, 24 March 1953, no. 16). The date on a signed church interior in the Hans Wetzlar collection, Amsterdam, was read as 162.(?); see sale, Sotheby Mak van Waay, Amsterdam, 9 June 1977, no. 277 (illus.). Grimmer's interest in ecclesiastical architecture is demonstrated not only by his paintings, but also by two drawings of church facades; see P. Genard, "Les Architectes anversois du XVIIe siècle," *Bulletin de l'Académie royale d'archéologie de Belgique,* 1882, p. 413.

2 A larger painting (panel, 50 x 66 cm), which appears to be a pastiche of this painting, was sold as "style of Pieter Neeffs" in the Von Kilenyi sale, Ernst-Museum, Budapest, 26 November 1917, no. 91 (illus.). In the Budapest painting, the nave appears narrower and includes more of the wall at the left, as well as variations in the staffage.

3 The clergyman in the right foreground appears in another signed church interior (Sotheby's, London, 8 April 1981, no. 138) and the peasant (gypsy?) woman and child in the foreground with their backs to the viewer are similar to figures in the foreground of Grimmer's *Christ on the Way to Calvary,* signed and dated 1599 (Birmingham Museum of Art, Alabama).

4 The authorship of the figures has not been established. On the subject of Grimmer's collaboration in architectural painting, see Legrand, "Abel Grimmer," pp. 163–67.

5 Other legible tomb inscriptions include: *HIER LIET BEGRAVEN/MARTEN DEVRIES/…; ELIE BODEL…/…; D O M* (Deus Optimus Maximus).

Cornelis de Heem 1631–1695

17

Still Life with Fruit
Oil on canvas, 44.7 x 37.3 cm

Born in Leiden, Cornelis de Heem studied with his father, Jan Davidsz. de Heem, one of the seventeenth century's greatest still-life painters. Just a boy when his father moved to Antwerp in 1636, he appears to have spent most of his life there, except for a stay in The Hague around 1677 or 1678. Cornelis enjoyed early success, being one of the youngest artists cited in Cornelis de Bie's *Het gulden cabinet* published in Antwerp in 1661, one year after De Heem became a master in the painters' guild.[1] Devoted entirely to still life, he painted a large number of works, often making variations on the same motif. This painting, for example, should be compared with another by him (fig. 17a), which, although slightly larger and more elaborate, is essentially the same composition.[2]

In this work, De Heem uses brilliant colors against a dark background to stress the jewel-like quality of the fruits. With their luminous tones and strong highlights, the cherries and grapes appear to be made of glass. Equally artificial is the composition; the large, red plum, for example, is precariously balanced on the apricots at the right. De Heem's sacrifice of realism for decorative effect is indicative of the direction still-life painting took during the second half of the seventeenth century.

17a De Heem, *Fruit Still Life with a Glass of Wine,* canvas, 42 x 50 cm. Private collection, Bergamo, Italy

Signed on stone ledge *C DE·HEEM·*

Provenance: Christie's, London, 22 November 1935, no. 114; Capt. E. G. Spencer-Churchill, M.C., Northwick Park; sale, Christie's, London, 29 October 1965, no. 51 (illus.); bought by J. McGowan; sale, Sotheby's, London, 10 July 1974, no. 48 (illus.); dealer, Parviz; dealer, Herner Wengraf, London, 1974; dealer, Parviz; sale, Sotheby Parke Bernet, N.Y., 11 June 1981, no. 32; private collection.

Reference: E.G.Spencer-Churchill, *Northwick Rescues 1912–1961* (Evesham: Sharp Bros., 1961), no. 13.

Exhibition: *VIIe biennale internationale,* Centre International de Paris, Porte Maillot, 3–20 October 1974, p. 316 (illus.).

1 C. de Bie, *Het gulden cabinet* ... (Antwerp: J. Meyssens, 1661), p. 369.

2 The other painting (canvas, 42 x 50 cm) is also signed. See I. Bergström, *La Natura in posa* ... (Bergamo: Galleria Lorenzelli, 1971), no. 26.

Jan Josef Horemans the Younger *1714–after 1790*

18

The Newborn
Oil on canvas, 47 x 62 cm

Of all the branches of painting, it was genre that enjoyed the greatest popularity in Antwerp during the eighteenth century. Scenes of everyday life were greatly influenced by paintings from the preceding century, in particular the work of Brouwer and Teniers. The later artists' admiration for and dependence upon the earlier masters is well illustrated in this mid-eighteenth-century painting by Jan Josef Horemans the Younger, a member of one of Antwerp's leading families of genre painters.

This scene depicts a social gathering connected with the birth of a child. The mother, still recovering in the canopied bed behind, looks out at two couples and a child who have come to see the new arrival, who is being fed by a dry-nurse near the fire. At the other side of the fireplace sits an old woman, undoubtedly the grandmother. Her black head covering indicates she is a widow. Originally the painting was accompanied by a pendant showing a similar group of people gathered around a table to celebrate a birth (fig. 18a).[1]

In these two pictures Horemans works in a seventeenth-century manner based on his observation of old paintings.[2] His main source was a large work entitled *The Ball* (fig. 18b), painted in 1658 by the Antwerp artist Hieronymus Janssens. The two visiting couples in *The Newborn* were both taken from Janssens's painting, where they appear in reversed order at the left. In the pendant to *The Newborn*, Horemans also includes one of the women and a child from the other side of the Janssens painting and uses them as his main figures. These same figures appear in other paintings by Horemans; the standing couple, for example, was repeated by him in at least four other works. In one dated 1763 (fig. 18c),[3] they again appear with the seated couple and, like them, are shown in reverse.[4] Horemans may have once owned the Janssens painting, he borrowed so extensively from it.[5] He also took from the paintings of other seventeenth-century artists, however, sometimes copying the entire work.[6]

The Newborn also bears a strong compositional relationship to several paintings by Janssens of the same subject, one of which is illustrated here (fig. 18d).[7] Ironically, it is the seventeenth-century painting with its very soft, delicate, and slightly attenuated figures that is more eighteenth century in spirit than

18a Horemans the Younger, *Presenting the Newborn*, canvas, 47 x 62 cm. Present whereabouts unknown (the illustration is from the F. Muller sale catalogue of 1900)

18b Hieronymus Janssens, Flemish, 1624–1693, *The Ball*, 1658, canvas, 112 x 168 cm. Musée des Beaux-Arts, Lille, France

18c Horemans the Younger, *Dining in the Garden*, 1763, canvas, 88.5 x 75.5 cm. Private collection (photo: RKD)

the Horemans painting, which is actually from the period. Not surprisingly, Janssens's paintings were very popular during the eighteenth century, and his *Ball* appears to have been the inspiration for Watteau's *Pleasures of the Ball* painted in 1719.[8]

Since there has been much confusion between the works of Jan Josef Horemans the Younger and his father, Jan Josef Horemans the Elder,[9] it is interesting to compare *The Newborn* with a painting of the same subject by the father (fig. 18e). In their composition, both paintings seem to have been influenced by Janssens, but the father dresses the figures in the costume of his own

18d Janssens, *The Newborn*, canvas, 86 x
124 cm. Present whereabouts unknown
(photo: RKD)

18e J.J. Horemans the Elder, Flemish,
1682–1759, *Visit to the Newborn*, 1727,
canvas, 48 x 56 cm. Present whereabouts
unknown (photo: RKD)

time. The son's palette is lighter and more colorful and he is less refined in his handling of form. Frequent borrowing of figures from seventeenth-century paintings also seems to be characteristic of the son rather than the father.[10]

Horemans's *Newborn* and its pendant document some of the Netherlandish traditions connected with the birth of a baby. The child who has come to see the newborn holds a toy windmill and a cone-shaped sack. The latter probably contains the so-called *kindermaandstik*, a confection that is still customarily presented to children on the occasion of a birth.[11] In the pendant, one of the men raises a glass to toast the new arrival. This tradition is explained in an old Dutch rhyme:

When the baby came into the world	Toen 't kindje op de wereld kwam,
From his niche so black,	Al uit zijn donker hoekje,
The friends drank mulled wine	Toen dronken de vrienden wijnkandeel,
And placed him in a wrap.	En ze wonden 't in een doekje.[12]

The Newborn also includes a *bakermat,* the curious wicker-basket seat in which the dry-nurse, or *baker,* sits while caring for the baby.[13] Here we see only the back of the *bakermat;* the front, which is lower, extends forward to contain the entire figure. Although the *bakermat* has long since gone out of use, the word still survives in Dutch and Flemish as a synonym for birthplace.

Signed lower right *J. Horemans.*

Verso: Two labels, one inscribed *175-154d¹/₂/cat. 5313/Horemans;* the other *175.* Number on stretcher *81821.*

Provenance: H.I.A. van Oldenbarnevelt, The Hague; sale, Frederik Muller, Amsterdam, 6–9 November 1900, no. 53, with pendant, as by J.J. Horemans I (illus.); Blakeslee Collection sale, American Art Galleries, N.Y., 10–11 April 1902, no. 133, with pendant no. 134, as by J.J. Horemans I, bought by Brunning; O'Reilly's Plaza Art Galleries, N.Y., 28 March 1968, no. 60 (*The Convalescent*), as by J.J. Horemans I; private collection.

---

1 The two paintings, unfortunately now separated, were last recorded together in a New York sale of 1902. A second pair of paintings, showing virtually the same two compositions, were in a Drouot sale in Paris, 28–29 June 1926, no. 209 (canvas, 48 x 58 cm; illus.). These paintings, which were recorded as signed, were attributed to Horemans's uncle Pieter Jacob Horemans (1700–1776). One difference between the two pairs is that the latter set does not include the leather wall covering, but does have a patterned fabric on both the bed and the fireplace valance.

2 It was noted in the Muller sale of 1900 (see above) that the costumes in Horemans's two paintings are from the seventeenth century.

3 The others include: 1) *A Dinner Party,* signed and dated 1754 (Cramer, The Hague, 1970–71, cat. 16, no. 85); 2) *Musical Group,* canvas, 46 x 58 cm, Wätjen sale, Hecht, Charlottenburg, 2–3 October 1928, no. 698 (illus.); 3) *Banquet Scene,* 47 x 54.6 cm, Morton sale, Christie's, 8 June 1928, no. 73. In the last painting, the couple is shown seated at a table. The seated woman in *The Newborn* also occupies a central position in a signed Horemans painting last recorded with the Galerie F. Kleinberger, Paris (photo: Louvre).

4 These were not the only figures that Horemans took from Janssens's *Ball.* The woman in the right foreground with her back to the viewer appears in a painting formerly with Von Diemen, Berlin, and several of the other figures, including the musician with the bass viol at the upper left, appear in *A Dinner Party* (see n. 3).

Some of the other figures in Horemans's *Newborn* and its pendant were also repeated in other works by him. The nurse holding the child, for example, appears in another painting, which, like *The Newborn,* has a pendant with a related theme. Both paintings were sold by Sotheby's, London, 10 December 1980, no. 1 (illus.). The man shown raising the glass in the pendant to *The Newborn* also appears in *Banquet Scene* (see n. 3).

5 The painting was acquired by the Lille Museum in 1873 as the bequest of A. Leleux.

6 For example, Horemans took the figures of Teniers, his wife, and his son from one of Teniers's two *Family Portraits* (Staatliche Museen, West Berlin, no. 857 and private collection, England) and used them in his *Musical Group* (see n. 3). Horemans's *Sausagemakers* (Coll. Earl of Bradford, Weston Park) is a direct copy of a painting by Teniers.

7 This painting, once attributed to Gonzales Coques, was formerly in the P. J. van Wijngaerdt collection, sale Roos, Amsterdam, 7 November 1893, no. 21. Of the other two paintings, one was formerly attributed to Anthonie Palamedesz (Coll. Charles T. Yerkes, Woodmere Art Gallery, Philadelphia, no. 140), the other to Philip van Dijck (Coll. Mme Poullier-Ketele, Brussels; sale, Leroy Frères, 23 March 1924, no. 8).

8 Dulwich College Picture Gallery. The connection between these two paintings was first noted by F.-C. Legrand, *Les Peintres flamands de genre au XVIIe siècle* (Brussels: Meddens, 1963), p. 88. See also O. T. Banks, *Watteau and the North: Studies in the Dutch and Flemish Baroque Influence on French Rococo Painting* (New York: Garland, 1977), pp. 211–12.

9 The confusion is compounded by the fact that both artists signed their paintings in the same way: J. Horemans.

10 One painting, *Dining in the Garden* (fig. 18c), bears the date 1763, which is four years after the father's death.

11 For a discussion of the meaning of the term *kindermaandstik* and its tradition, see G.D.J. Schotel, *Het oud-Hollandsche huisgezin der zeventiende eeuw* (Leiden: H. C. Rogge, 1904), pp. 34–35. Today the *kindermaandstik* is usually a buttered rusk topped with colored, sugar-coated anise seeds.

12 The entire rhyme is given in J. van Vloten, *Nederlandsche baker- en kinderrijmen* (Leiden: Sijthoff, 1894, facs. reprint 1969), p. 1.

13 For a discussion and illustrations of the *bakermat,* see A. Knoppers, *In de kraam: Wetenswaardigheden over oud-nederlandse kraamgebruiken* (Zoetermeer: Nutricia, 1975), pp. 14–15.

Pieter van der Hulst I *before 1575–1628?*

19

Italian Landscape with Ruins
Oil on panel, 56 x 84.3 cm

Pieter van der Hulst, who is thought to have been born in Malines, was registered as a master in the Antwerp guild in 1589. During the following decade, he had numerous pupils, including Jan Wildens in 1598. The few signed works by him are all landscapes or genre scenes painted in a very fluid style. This painting, which has only recently been attributed to him, includes an Antwerp guild mark on the back (fig. 19a).[1]

Italian Landscape with Ruins may be compared with the artist's *Village Kermis* of 1628 in the Brunswick Museum (fig. 19b).[2] Both pictures exhibit his characteristic treatment of foliage, which has a puffy, cloud-like appearance. The figures and animals are all greatly stylized and look almost toy-like. Particularly amusing in *Italian Landscape* are the cattle, two of which are partially hidden by shrubbery in the center and appear as one extremely long animal. Among the birds represented are several mallards and a hoopoe perched on a branch in the foreground. The branch in the water, on which another bird sits, is used to secure a basket-like cage in which fish are kept.

In both paintings, the architecture is treated in a summary and painterly fashion. Unlike the kermis scene, which shows contemporary, Netherlandish buildings, this work features ancient Roman structures: the large ruins and the round building in the distance. It is not known if Van der Hulst ever traveled to Italy; his antique architecture may have been inspired by the work of the many Flemish artists who did. And though Italian in subject, his landscape is typically Flemish in the way it is composed, with three distinct spatial divisions of foreground, middle-ground, and background. The lighted areas are characterized by a rich mixture of color, which serves to counterbalance the bold brushwork.

19a Brand of Antwerp

19b Van der Hulst, *Village Kermis*, 1628, panel, 49.4 x 92.5 cm. Herzog Anton Ulrich-Museum, Brunswick, West Germany

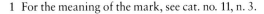

Verso: Brand of Antwerp (height 5.5 cm) and in black paint *N˚ 1455*.

Provenance: M. Darieutort, Paris, 1973; dealer, S. Nystad, The Hague; sale, Sotheby's, London, 16 July 1980, no. 255, as by Willem van Nieulandt; Douwes Fine Art, London, 1981; private collection.

Exhibition: *28ste oude kunst- en antiekbeurs,* Stedelijk Museum "Het Prinsenhof," Delft, 14 October – 3 November 1976.

1 For the meaning of the mark, see cat. no. 11, n. 3.

2 The Brunswick painting is signed *.P. V. HVLST. 1628*.

Pieter Huys   *ca. 1519–1584*

20

Woman Enraged
Oil on panel, 64.8 x 50 cm

In *Woman Enraged* we are confronted by a bizarrely attired, screaming female. Although clearly an unusual character, the woman cannot be identified with any known literary or historical figure. As we shall see, the painting appears to be an allegory with moralistic overtones.

To appreciate the painting's significance, it is helpful to compare it with one of Pieter Huys's other works, *The Bagpiper* of 1571 (fig. 20a).[1] An inscription at the top of *The Bagpiper* documents its moralistic message. The loose living symbolized by drinking and music making have come to an end, as the old woman removes the empty purse from her unhappy companion. The bagpipe and pitcher, both sexual symbols, add to the bawdy meaning: the deflated instrument implies that the man can no longer fulfill the woman's sexual desires, symbolized by the pitcher.[2]

20a Huys, *The Bagpiper*, 1571, panel, 86 x 84 cm. Staatliche Museen, East Berlin

Although it bears no inscription, *Woman Enraged* also conveys a message through the use of symbols. The woman's expression clearly indicates anger. Through the door behind her, we catch a glimpse of a fireplace, which may well be an allusion to anger, for fire is the element traditionally associated with the choleric temperament.

In addition to Anger, the figure personifies Avarice, as seen from her eclectic attire and possessions. Part of her costume is similar to that worn by the woman in *The Bagpiper:* a white headdress and underblouse and a red-and-blue bodice with separate red outer sleeves, which are pinned at the shoulder. Added to this are several incongruous items. The straw hat is that of a peasant and is not normally worn indoors (see p. 103). It symbolizes the lower-class nature of our subject and forms a striking contrast to her black, sleeveless robe, which is apparently made of velvet and fitted with a scallop collar. Attached to the robe are some gold rings, and around the woman's neck hangs a string of red and gold beads – possibly a rosary – and an ornate, gold-and-silver chain and medallion. In addition to what she wears, the woman holds on her right arm a white cloth or garment, and on her left, a fashionable piece of clothing made of blue fabric with a yellow lining and white laces. She also holds an earthenware jug in almost the same manner as the woman in *The Bagpiper.*

It is the incongruity of the peasant woman and her ill-assorted finery that symbolizes Avarice. The jug she holds also suggests that her covetousness is not limited to material possessions, but includes gluttony and sexual appetite. As a symbol of drinking, the jug relates to both greed and anger – especially prolonged anger – two vices often associated with drunkenness.[3]

Huys's *Woman Enraged* calls to mind the main figure in Pieter Brueghel's *Dulle Griet,* painted around 1562. There have been numerous interpretations of this legendary character (fig. 20b); central to all, however, are the anger and greed that are conveyed by her actions and material possessions. Like Huys's enraged woman, Dulle Griet is ruled by her emotions; here she even attempts to storm hell to gain her loot.

Anger and Avarice are two of the Seven Deadly Sins, a common subject in sixteenth-century Flemish art. Artists like Brueghel created extremely powerful images to show how man could become a victim of his vices.[4] Huys's *Woman Enraged* is certainly no exception. It commands attention while it condemns. The painting's many levels of meaning would have appealed to members of Antwerp's intellectual community.

Brueghel's and Huys's use of a woman to portray vice reflect a contemporary attitude that women were inferior to men morally and intellectually and were also extremely susceptible to vices like ill-temper and extravagance. This age-old prejudice was reinforced by a wave of anti-feminism that reached its height in Europe around the middle of the sixteenth century.[5]

When radiographs were made recently of *Woman Enraged,* it was discovered that it had been painted on top of another work depicting the Holy Family. The earlier painting shows the Madonna holding the Christ Child on her lap, with Saint Joseph appearing farther back at the left (figs. 20c, 20d). On the Madonna's lap is a book, which she holds with her left hand. The image appears to date from the early sixteenth century and thus is the work of another artist.[6]

It may seem surprising that Huys obliterated a sacred subject with his aggressive and caustic image, yet one must consider the period in which he was working. In the years around 1670, the approximate date of *Woman Enraged,* Protestant opposition to sacred art reached a peak in a series of riots that denuded many churches of their paintings. At this time, religious works may well have been sold for the worth of the panels on which they were painted. And of course, as a moralistic image, Huys's *Woman Enraged* is actually much more suited to Protestant thought.

20b Pieter Brueghel the Elder, Flemish, 1525-30–1569, detail of *Dulle Griet,* panel, 115 x 161 cm. Museum Mayer van den Bergh, Antwerp (photo: A.C.L., Brussels)

20c Radiograph of *Woman Enraged*

20d Line drawing of the painting beneath *Woman Enraged,* traced from the radiograph

Verso: Printed paper label *THE MUSTARD WOMAN.*[7]*/ RESTORED BY W. & P. EVANS/ JUNE 1883.*

Provenance: Restored by William & Philip Evans, London, 1883;[8] Central Picture Galleries, N.Y., 1962; private collection.

---

1 The attribution of *Woman Enraged* is based on its strong connections to *The Bagpiper.* The figures in both paintings show a strikingly similar physiognomy, in particular the distinctive, long-fingered hands. The settings are also basically the same: a window at the left and door at the right.

The Bagpiper is one of only four signed works by Huys. The other three are religious subjects in the style of Hieronymus Bosch: *The Temptation of Saint Anthony,* 1547, panel, 71 x 102.5 cm, Louvre, Paris; *Inferno,* 1570, panel, 86 x 82 cm, Prado, Madrid; *The Temptation of Saint Anthony,* 1577, panel, 77 x 93.9 cm, Museum Mayer van den Bergh, Antwerp.

2 For further discussion of the symbolism, see H. Mund, "La Peinture de moeurs chez Pieter Huys,"*Revue des archéologues et historiens d'art de Louvain* 13 (1980): 64–73.

3 See M. A. Sullivan, "Madness and Folly: Peter Bruegel the Elder's *Dulle Griet,*" *Art Bulletin* 59 (March 1977): 55–66, esp. p. 63.

4 Brueghel's famous print series of *The Seven Deadly Sins* appeared in 1558.

5 See W. S. Gibson, "Bruegel, Dulle Griet, and Sexist Politics in the Sixteenth Century," in *Pieter Bruegel und seine Welt* (Berlin: Gebr. Mann Verlag, 1979), pp. 9–15.

6 A few small losses in the upper layer of paint revealed that the robe of the Madonna underneath is red. Close examples of this type of image date from the 1520s and 1530s. Compositionally, the painting of the Holy Family gives the appearance of being somewhat truncated at the left side (note in particular Saint Joseph), suggesting that Huys may have trimmed the panel to accommodate his design. This suggestion is supported by the fact that the left edge is the only one that does not include a bevel on the reverse.

7 This English title seems to derive from the woman's enraged expression. Whether the title was a 19th-century invention or a translation of an original Flemish one is unknown. If it does originate from the Low Countries, it may relate to the expression *iemand door den mosterd sleepen,* literally "to drag someone through the mustard," that is to scold or rake someone over the coals.

8 In the 1883 London post-office directory, William and Philip Evans were listed as "gilders & picture restorers" located at 18 Silver Street, Golden Square.

Jan van Kessel the Elder 1626–1679
Erasmus Quellinus II 1607–1678

21

Allegory of Europe, 1670
Oil on copper attached to cradle, 49.5 x 68.5 cm

Jan van Kessel, son of the portrait painter Hieronymus van Kessel, was related to several of Antwerp's best-known artists. He was the grandson of Jan Brueghel the Elder and nephew of Jan Brueghel the Younger and David Teniers the Younger. He was apprenticed to the genre and history painter Simon de Vos and may also have studied with his uncle Jan Brueghel. Van Kessel became a master in the Antwerp guild in 1645. A specialist in painting animals, insects, and plants, he often collaborated with other artists, as in this work in which the three foreground figures appear to be by Erasmus Quellinus II.

This colorful allegory is closely related to one that Van Kessel completed six years earlier as part of a series on the four regions of the world, the complete set of which is in the Alte Pinakothek, Munich (fig. 21a). Executed between 1664 and 1666, the series comprises four paintings the same size as this work, each framed by sixteen smaller paintings that illustrate in encyclopedic fashion the towns and animals indigenous to the different regions.[1] The figures in the four main paintings are also attributed to Quellinus.

Representations of the four parts of the world came into vogue about a century before Van Kessel's series. The explorations of the sixteenth century helped not only to replace the tripartite image of the world—Europe, Asia, Africa—with the concept of four continents, but also to establish Europe's superiority. These allegorical images served both the state and the church—particularly the latter, which, during the Counter Reformation, used them to denote its world-wide influence.[2]

In the painting exhibited here, as in the one in Munich, Europe is represented as a woman wearing an ermine-lined cape and a crown with a cross. In her right hand she displays a small gold statue of victory,[3] and next to her are two angels holding paintings. The ecclesiastical figures behind her signify her spiritual leadership. The pope is shown in a room at the back receiving a dignitary, a reference to the church's preeminent position (fig. 21b). Several cardinals look on, while another walks in the arcade at the right. In the far distance is Castel Sant'Angelo, long associated with the papacy and also a symbol of Rome, Europe's most important city at this time. At the top of the stairs are statues of Peter and Paul, founders of the Christian Church.

J.V. Kessel, fecit A°
1670

21a Van Kessel, *Europe,* 1664, copper, central panel, 48.5 x 67.5 cm; small panels, each 14.5 x 21 cm. Alte Pinakothek, Munich

Europe's secular leadership is represented by portraits incorporated in the walls of the palatial setting. The most powerful ruler at the time, Louis XIV, occupies a prominent position over the doorway at the back. On the front wall are, from left to right, Charles II of England, Charles II of Spain, Leopold I, Holy Roman Emperor, and Juan Dominico Zuniga, governor of the Spanish Netherlands. All of the portraits are identified by inscriptions at the top.

Van Kessel also includes several paintings of the type for which he is best known: three of insects, one of animals (a pair of flamingos), and a large floral still life—all of which suggest Europe's leading role in the natural sciences. So detailed are these paintings that it is possible to identify in the three insect pictures more than four dozen species, as well as others that appear in the flower painting.[4] Nevertheless, none of these pictures can be associated with original paintings; they apparently were designed specifically for the allegory. This also seems to be the case with the two still lifes on the back wall, which are made up of many of the same objects scattered around the room in the Munich painting (fig. 21a). The one on the left with an artist's palette and a globe symbolizes Europe's role in the arts and sciences. The other refers to her secular and religious leadership and includes both military

21b Detail of *Allegory of Europe*

and sacred objects, among them the Bible and a papal bull, both with partially legible texts.[5] Europe's superiority in the arts and commerce is also symbolized by the statues of Minerva and Mercury at the base of the stairs.

The array of military equipment at the lower left represents Europe's supremacy in war. The objects range from a suit of jousting armor of the late fifteenth or early sixteenth century to a pair of lion-headed pistols of around 1640.[6] Also strewn across the floor are a variety of sea shells, which again point to Europe's interest in the natural sciences. Some of them are from waters far from Europe and suggest her world-wide exploration. A more obvious example of her contact with other parts of the world is the Turkish carpet covering the dais on which Europe sits.

Van Kessel's painting is more than an allegorical representation; it is a *Wunderkammer,* a room in which both works of art and natural curiosities are displayed. Paintings of animals, insects, and flowers showing the wonders of nature were particularly appropriate to a *Wunderkammer.* These collections must have delighted Van Kessel, who so often took an encyclopedic approach to his subjects. His two versions of the allegory of Europe suggest the pleasure he derived from painting images of such great detail.

Signed lower right *I.V. Kessel, fecit A°/1670*

Provenance: Purchased in Manhattan; private collection.

1 For a study of these paintings, see the exhibition catalogue by U. Krempel, *Jan van Kessel d. Ä. 1626–1679: Die vier Erdteile,* 8 May–30 September 1973, Alte Pinakothek, Munich. See also I. Bergström, et al., *Natura in posa: La grande stagione della natura morta europea* (Milan: Rizzoli, 1977), p. 63, and *Stilleben in Europa,* exh. cat. (Münster: Westfälisches Landesmuseum, 1979), pp. 38ff.

2 See H. Honour, *The New Golden Land: European Images of America from the Discoveries to the Present Time* (New York: Pantheon, 1975), pp. 84–117.

3 Judging from a pentimento, the victory figure was originally farther to the left.

4 Not all the representations are completely accurate. For example, one of the insects has eight legs. I am grateful to members of the Entomological Society of the Royal Zoological Society of Antwerp for their identifications of the insects.

5 The inscription on the Bible is the same as in the Munich painting: *BIBLIA/Ad Veriestissima* (sic)/ *exemplarie/castigata/QUID in horum*/(Bibliovum)/*castigatio*(ne); the papal bull is inscribed *CLEMENS./PP.VIII/ADFVTARAM* (sic) *REI/MEMORIAM./...24... /CAPELLO.BISS/datum 1670* (?). This text is basically the same as on the papal bull in the Munich painting except for the name Alexander VII, who was pope at the time. Clement VIII probably refers to Clement IX (or VIIII), who succeeded Alexander VII and was pope until 9 December 1669. The next pope, Clement X, was not elected until 29 April 1670.

6 I am grateful to Walter J. Karcheski of the Higgins Armory Museum for identifying the military equipment.

Adriaen Thomas Key *ca. 1544–after 1589*

22

Portrait of a Gentleman, 1572
Oil on panel, 40.6 x 34.3 cm, transferred to a cradled panel 47 x 37.7 cm

During the sixteenth century, portrait painting in Flanders took on a much more expressive quality than in the preceding century. Influenced by Italian Renaissance portraiture, Flemish artists sought to convey not only the physical appearance, but also the personality of the sitter.

This portrait, long associated with Frans Pourbus the Elder, is here attributed to a contemporary, Adriaen Thomas Key. The rich coloring and soft, almost silky quality of the skin is characteristic of Key's early style. At this time, he was still strongly influenced by the portraitist Willem Key, thought to be his uncle and one of his teachers. Although the modeling in this portrait is soft, the artist powerfully conveys the sculptural mass of the head. Details like the lines across the forehead and around the eyes help reveal the character of the unknown sitter.

At the top of the painting are two inscriptions: the date of the work and the man's age.[1] The painting, which has been transferred to another panel, appears to have been trimmed, but the original composition was probably not much bigger.[2] On his large portraits, Key placed his inscriptions near the edge of the panel, not close to the head as seen here.[3]

Inscribed upper left *(1)572* and upper right *AE TA•4(?)*.

Provenance: Sale, Jos. Fiévez, Brussels, 12–13 July 1905, no. 100, as school of Pourbus (illus.); Christie's, N.Y., 12 January 1978, no. 114, as by Frans Pourbus the Elder (illus.); private collection.

1 The second digit of the sitter's age is no longer legible; however, in a 1905 sale, the age was read as 41.

2 The excess of the larger panel, now concealed by the frame, was until recently painted to look like part of the original.

3 See, for example, his signed, half-length portrait from the same year in the Kunsthistorisches Museum, Vienna (no. 3679).

Quentin Massys *1465-66–1530*

23

Allegory of Folly
Oil on panel, 60 x 47.3 cm

Quentin Massys is one of the first major artists of the Antwerp School. A native of Louvain, he entered the Antwerp painters' guild in 1491 and soon became the town's leading artist and teacher. More than anyone else, he effected the transition there from the native Flemish tradition to a style influenced by the Italian Renaissance. Massys was particularly attracted to the work of Leonardo da Vinci. Leonardo's grotesque head studies may well have influenced this powerful, satirical image, thought to have been painted around 1510.

Massys's peculiar figure wears the traditional costume of the fool consisting of bells and a cowl with ass ears and a cock's head. At the time the work was painted, professional fools were still very common. Often a member of the royal court, the fool was also seen in morality plays and at carnivals. The court fool was sometimes a mentally deficient person whose antics provided amusement. More often, however, he was a comedian who used the guise of foolishness as a vehicle for wit and satire.

23a *Allegory of Folly* before cleaning

Massys's character holds a long stick topped by a small, armless figure who also wears a fool's cap. This object, known as a marotte or bauble, was used for humorous or satirical dialogue much like a ventriloquist's dummy. The marotte's obscene gesture, which symbolizes the insults associated with the fool,[1] was apparently considered distasteful by a previous owner, for the figure was once painted over, as seen in an earlier photo (fig. 23a).

The grotesque nature of Massys's figure makes it impossible to ascertain whether it is male or female. Like many artists, Massys suggests abnormal character through physical deformities like a hunched back and large, hooked nose.[2] The wen, which appears on the forehead, was associated with stupidity and feeble-mindedness and was believed to contain the so-called stone of folly that was responsible for a fool's mental condition.[3]

Fools were a popular subject in art and literature of the sixteenth century and, as in this painting, were often used as a symbol of Folly. Massys's picture is almost contemporary with Erasmus's *Praise of Folly* (1509), in which Folly, represented as a woman, becomes the moral commentator on the follies of others.[4] Erasmus, who had a strong influence on Antwerp humanists and whose portrait was painted by Massys, praised the candid nature of Folly, who through humor is able to impart unpleasant truths. The stone of folly and overall grotesque appearance of this fool, however, implies the figure is not a wise satirist, the book stashed in his bag no symbol of knowledge.

The fool's gesture of silence can be traced back to the Greek god of silence, Harpocrates, who was also shown with his index finger to his lips. Long associated with wisdom and eloquence, silence or restrained speech was usually considered a trait of the philosopher, scholar, or monk.[5] This association was very common in the sixteenth century, as we see in a woodcut of 1522 showing a scholar with his finger pressed to his lips (fig. 23b). In Massys's painting, the gesture is combined with the inscription *Mondeken toe,* "keep your mouth shut"; the cock cackling away overhead, however, represents the fool's inability to remain silent—in other words, "fools will talk." A similar image is provided by a woodcut that appeared in Sebastian Brant's *Ship of Fools* (fig. 23c). Here a fool with his tongue out, a gesture repeated by his marotte, indicates lack of discretion. He is compared to the woodpecker, whose constant "chatter" reveals the nest containing his young.[6]

The inscription *Mondeken toe* is combined with the word *Mot,* which is a later addition.[7] The word has various translations. Here it probably refers to an immoral woman or whore, one of the meanings it had during the sixteenth and seventeenth centuries.[8] The addition suggests that someone wished to turn Massys's fool into an equally notorious character, a procuress or madame.

23b *Silence,* trademark of Thomas Wolff, 1522, woodcut (photo: Houghton Library, Harvard University)

Inscribed upper left *Mot./Mondeken/toe.*

Provenance: Miss Norah Smith, Montreal, as by Pieter Brueghel, 1938; Coll. Mr. and Mrs. Julius S. Held.

Exhibitions: *The Worcester-Philadelphia Exhibition of Flemish Painting,* Worcester Art Museum, 23 February–12 March 1939, J. G. Johnson Collection at the Philadelphia Museum of Art, 25 March–26 April 1939, no. 45 *(The Fool); Masterpieces of Dutch Art,* Grand Rapids Art Gallery, Grand Rapids, Mich., 7–30 May 1940, no. 45 *(The Fool); Holbein and His Contemporaries,* John Herron Art Museum, Indianapolis, Ind., 22 October–24 December 1950, no. 50 (illus.); *Sixteenth Century Paintings from American Collections,* Vassar College Art Gallery, Poughkeepsie, N.Y., 16 October–15 November 1964, no. 8; *Paintings and Sculpture from the Collection of Mr. and Mrs. Julius S. Held,* Smith College Museum of Art, Northampton, Mass., 1–27 October 1968, no. 33.

References: *Art in America* 27 (July 1939): 147 (illus.); *Art News Annual* 37, no. 22 (1939): 56 (illus.); M. L. Wilson, *The Tragedy of Hamlet Told by Horatio* (Enschede: De Viking, 1956), pp. 621–22, fig. 83; E. Tietze-Conrat, *Dwarfs and Jesters in Art* (London: Phaidon Press, 1957), pp. 19, 94, fig. 21; W. Willeford, *The Fool and His Scepter* (Evanston: Northwestern University Press, 1969), pp. 6, 29, pl. 2; L. A. Silver, "Quentin Massys (1466–1530)" (Ph.D. diss., Harvard University, 1974), pp. 214–15, 355–56; A. de Bosque, *Quentin Metsys* (Brussels: Arcade, 1975), pp. 196, no. 242 (illus.) attr. to Massys; S. Poley, *Unter der Maske des Narren* (Stuttgart: Hatje, 1981), p. 47, fig. 39.

23c Woodcut from Sebastian Brant's *Ship of Fools* (photo: Houghton Library, Harvard University)

1 For a discussion of this gesture, see J. Gessler, "A propos d'un acteur dans le Jeu de sainte Apolline," in *Miscellanea Leo van Puyvelde* (Brussels: Éditions de la Connaissance, 1949), pp. 269–76.

2 See Willeford, *The Fool and His Scepter,* p. 14.

3 The removal of this stone was considered a cure for folly. There are numerous paintings of this fictitious operation including one by Hieronymus Bosch (ca. 1475–80) and one by Jan Sanders van Hemessen (1555), both in the Prado.

4 The connections between Massys and Erasmus are discussed by Silver, "Massys," pp. 214–16, and C. Limentani Virdis, "Moralismo e satira nella tarda produzione di Quentin Metsys," *Storia dell'arte* 20 (1974): 19–24. See also G. Marlier, *Erasme et la peinture flamande de son temps* (Damme: Musée van Maerlant, 1954).

5 See W. Deonna, "Le Silence, gardien du secret," *Zeitschrift für Schweizerische Archaeologie und Kunstgeschichte* 12 (1951): 28ff; and K. Langedijk, "Silentium," *Nederlands kunsthistorisch jaarboek* 15 (1964): 3–18.

6 I am grateful to William Robinson for furnishing me with material from his research on the silence gesture in 16th- and 17th-century Netherlandish art.

7 The word was painted over lightly so it would not detract from the painting's original appearance, yet it is still legible.

8 M. de Vries et al., eds., *Woordenboek der Nederlandsche taal* (The Hague: M. Nijhoff, 1882–), 9: cols. 1172f.

Monogrammist IHB

24

24a Jan Brueghel the Elder, Flemish, 1568–1625, and Hendrik van Balen, Flemish, 1575–1632, *Allegory of Fire*, panel, 55 x 93 cm. Galleria Doria Pamphili, Rome

Venus at the Forge of Vulcan, 1659
Oil on copper attached to a panel, 35.7 x 46.8 cm

Venus at the Forge of Vulcan derives from a composition painted around 1611 by Jan Brueghel the Elder (fig. 24a),[1] which was the inspiration for numerous works. The date of this version attests to the long-term popularity of the original design. The subject comes from Virgil's *Aeneid* (8:370-85), in which Venus asked her husband, Vulcan, to make armor for her son Aeneas, who was about to go to war in Latium. Brueghel's painting, which was part of a series on the Four Elements, uses the scene to represent fire. The same image could also be an allegory of love and war, however, and it is not known if either of these themes was intended here.

The monogram and date on this work are identical to those on a painting in Basel (fig. 24b). The artist, known today only by his monogram, had a distinctive style, particularly his use of small, short, parallel strokes, best seen in the foliage.[2] The main figures, Vulcan, Venus, and Cupid, are somewhat more refined than the others and may be by another hand, as in Brueghel's painting which has figures by Hendrik van Balen.

24b Monogrammist IHB, *Staghunt*, 1659, copper, 38.5 x 47.5 cm. Kunstmuseum, Basel

Venus at the Forge of Vulcan is a virtual *Wunderkammer*, with almost every product of the metal-working craft represented: jewelry, vessels, armor, and weapons, to name but a few. Also depicted are the actual production processes, from the gathering of raw materials to the final grinding and polishing. Particularly fascinating is the horse-powered device in the background that is being used to bore a hole in a large cannon.

Signed lower left on edge of bench *IHB 1659*

Provenance: Sale, A. Mak, Amsterdam, 18 March 1919, no. 7, as by Hendrik van Balen (illus.); private collection.

---

1 Brueghel himself painted several versions; see K. Ertz, *Jan Brueghel der Ältere...* (Cologne: DuMont, 1979), pp. 368–84.

2 The monogram was read as J.H.B. by J.J. Bachofen-Burckhardt; see her entry in the 1907 Basel catalogue, no. 51. It is not clear, however, whether the first letter is *J* or *I* or if the monogram should be read simply as *HB*. There are many unsigned works that appear to be by the same hand, such as no. 4995 in the Alte Pinakothek, Munich, which is also after a Brueghel composition (Ertz, *Brueghel*, no. 176).

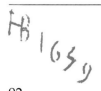

Pieter Neeffs I *ca. 1578–1656-61*
Frans Francken III *1607–1667*

25

Church Interior
Oil on panel, 24 x 34.5 cm

An example of the collaboration so common among Flemish artists of the seventeenth century, this church interior bears the signature of both Pieter Neeffs, who painted the architecture, and Frans Francken, who did the figures. Pieter Neeffs I and his son Pieter II often collaborated with Frans Franken II and his son Frans III. Understandably, it is often difficult to be sure which artists were responsible for a particular work, even when, like this one, it is signed by both. The Neeffs signature as it appears here could be that of the father or the son; however, the use of a fine, dark outline throughout the architecture suggests the work of the father. The figures, less refined than those of Frans Francken II, in particular the faces (see cat. nos. 12, 15), appear to be the work of his son.[1]

In some collaborative efforts it is not easy to determine the order in which the various parts were painted; in a work such as this one, however, it is clear that the figures, or staffage, were added after the architecture was completed, as proven in several places where the underlying design, such as the floor tiles, show through the figures because the upper layers of paint have become transparent with time. The architectural painter's dependency on the staffage painter is greater than one might at first think. Besides adding human interest and a sense of scale, the figures can also serve other important functions, as in this painting where two of them provide a main source of illumination – which ironically was added after the light effect was created.

Pieter Neeffs I painted numerous nocturnal scenes. In this church interior, which seems to be the artist's own invention, the light and shadow transform the severe, linear Gothic forms into an atmospheric, cave-like setting. Within this labyrinth, the artist, using a very simple palette of ocher and gray, creates a wide variety of coloristic effects, from the checker-board pattern of the floor to the very subtle candlelight against the walls.

There are several other paintings by Pieter Neeffs I showing virtually the same church interior; the one most similar, in the Prado (fig. 25a), is identical in size and has figures that also appear to be by Frans Francken III.[2] In both

94

25a Pieter Neeffs I and Frans Francken III, *Church Interior,* panel, 25 x 34 cm. Prado, Madrid

paintings the focus is on a small procession of women that makes its way from the shadowy nave into the brilliantly illuminated foreground. This procession, which does not appear to be a baptism, could be a visit by a distinguished lady, or possibly a churching, a ceremony by which a woman, after childbirth, is received back into the church.

Signed on wall at right *Peeter/Neeffs/ffranck*

Verso: A seal in red wax with a crown and the letters *LV* joined (Ludwig Viktor).

Provenance: Archduke Ludwig Viktor, Schloss Klessheim, Salzburg; sale, Dorotheum, Vienna, 30 May–3 June 1921, no. 129, as by Pieter Neeffs II and Frans Francken III (illus.); private collection, New Orleans; Mr. and Mrs. Eugene Bernat, Upton, Mass., 1982; Mr. William A. Bernat.

1 I am grateful to Ursula Kudszus Härting for her comments on this painting.

2 Other closely related works include: *Church Interior,* panel, 29 x 41 cm, Lazaro, Madrid, no. 11303; *Church Interior,* panel, 39 x 54 cm, Fleischner sale, Pisko, Vienna, 27–28 November 1905, no. 85 (illus.); *Church Interior,* panel, 25.7 x 39.7 cm, Johnson Collection, Philadelphia Museum of Art, no. 708 (catalogued as Pieter Neeffs II).

Frans Pourbus the Younger *1569–1622*

26

Maria de' Medici
Oil on copper, 5.4 x 4.2 cm (reproduced here twice its actual size)

A native of Antwerp, Frans Pourbus entered the painters' guild there in 1591. He eventually moved to Brussels, where he painted at the court of the Archduke Albert and Isabella. In 1600 he went to Italy to work for Vincenzo Gonzaga, Duke of Mantua. There he painted numerous portraits, many of which were for the duke's gallery of pictures of beautiful women. Pourbus remained in the duke's service until 1609, when he was called to Paris to become court painter to Maria de' Medici, a position he held until his death.

It was not uncommon to have a miniature painted in connection with a large-scale portrait, and this work shows the same likeness of Maria as one of Pourbus's large, full-length portraits formerly in the Rothan Collection, Paris (fig. 26a).[1] Burchard suggested that the large portrait may have resulted from the artist's visit to Paris in August and September 1606, when Pourbus was still in the service of Vincenzo Gonzaga.[2]

After he became court painter to Maria in 1609, Pourbus painted numerous additional portraits of her.[3] In 1616, for example, he was paid for executing three miniatures of the queen, two of which were made for other individuals.[4] And in 1617 he painted a miniature and two larger portraits, one of which was sent to Maria's daughter in Spain. The miniature was retained by the queen for her "pleasure and use."[5]

In 1606, when this work is thought to have been done, Maria was thirty-four years old and had been queen of France for six years. After her husband, Henry IV, was assassinated in 1610, she became regent for her son Louis XIII. An extremely active patron of the arts, Maria made a major contribution to early seventeenth-century painting in France by commissioning artists of the highest quality, regardless of their nationality or style. She distinguished herself by employing both Pourbus and Rubens, two of the finest Flemish painters of the day.

Pourbus dominated French portraiture during both the reign of Henry IV and the regency of Maria. His portraits, part of the late Mannerist tradition, are characterized by stiff poses and an emphasis on the extremely decorative costumes of the period. In this miniature, he pays careful attention to all the details of the queen's ornate dress, in particular her elaborate lace collar, which has been adjusted to fit the oval format. Through skillful modeling, he conveys the texture of the various fabrics, the hair, the skin, and the pearl necklaces and earring. Pourbus even used powdered-gold pigment for the latter as well as the elaborate ornaments on her dress and in her hair.

26a Pourbus, *Maria de' Medici*, canvas, 215 x 123 cm. Present whereabouts unknown (photo: A.C. Cooper, London)

The queen's jewelry and lavish costume, which to modern taste may seem excessive, were in fact part of royal etiquette. As Deborah Marrow has pointed out, magnificence was a desirable attribute for both a ruler and a woman.[6] It was a virtue for which Maria was praised both during her life and after.

Provenance: Dealer, Siegfried Rosenau, N.Y., 1962; Coll. Mr. and Mrs. Julius S. Held.

Exhibitions: *Paintings and Sculpture from the Collection of Mr. and Mrs. Julius S. Held*, Smith College Museum of Art, Northampton, Mass., 1–27 October 1968, no. 41; *Between the Lines: Ladies and Letters at the Clark*, Sterling and Francine Clark Art Institute, Williamstown, Mass., 20 March–25 April 1982.

1 Canvas, 215 x 123 cm. The Gustave Rothan portrait, which was engraved by H. Vion, was sold by Georges Petit, Paris, 29–31 May 1890, no. 88. It was next recorded in a Christie's sale on 1 June 1956 as the property of the Duke of Roxburghe, London, no. 32, *Portrait of a Lady*, attributed to M. Gheeraerts. The painting was purchased by Hallsborough. Its present location is unknown.

A bust-length portrait showing the same likeness of Maria was also in the Rothan collection sale, no. 89, canvas, 62 x 49 cm. A photo of this work made by Amsler and Ruthart, Vienna, is in the Rubenianum, Antwerp.

2 *Allgemeines Lexikon der bildenden Künstler,* s.v. "Frans Pourbus d.J.," p. 316.

3 Pourbus's other large portraits of Maria de' Medici are in the following collections: Palazzo Pitti, Florence (half-length), canvas, 80 x 61 cm, dated 1606; Louvre, Paris (full-length), canvas, 307 x 186 cm, signed, ca. 1609–10; Palazzo Riccardi, Florence (three-quarter length), canvas, 142 x 127 cm, signed and dated 1611; Prado, Madrid (full-length), canvas, 215 x 115 cm, signed and dated 1617.

4 This document, dated 31 December 1616, was published by M. J. J. Guiffrey in *Nouvelles Archives de l'art français,* ser. 2, 3 (1882): 13–14. For examples of other miniatures attributed to Pourbus, see P. Rosenberg and S. Maloni Trkulja, *Pittura francese nelle collezioni pubbliche fiorentine,* exh. cat. (Florence: Palazzo Pitti, 1977), pp. 257–58.

5 "Un petit à mettre dans une boeste, que nous avons retenu pour nostre plaisir et service." The document of this commission was first published by M. A. de Boislisle, "François Porbus, portraits de Marie de Médicis," *Nouvelles Archives de l'art français,* ser. 2, 1 (1879): 94.

6 D. Marrow, *The Art Patronage of Maria de' Medici* (Ann Arbor: UMI Research Press, 1982), pp. 58–59.

Marten Rijckaert *1587–1631*

27

Landscape with Windmill and Wayside Chapel
Oil on panel, 27.7 x 50.5 cm

Marten Rijckaert was the son of the painter David Rijckaert, with whom he probably first studied. He was also cited as a pupil of the landscape painter Tobias Verhaecht and as having traveled to Italy. In any case, he was back in Antwerp by 1611, the year he became a master in the painters' guild. By this time he had lost an arm, a handicap noted in Anthony van Dyck's *Iconography:* "Marten Rijckaert, one-armed, painter of rural views of Antwerp."[1]

Characteristic of Rijckaert's small, but multifaceted, panoramic scenes, this landscape combines elements from both within and outside the Netherlands: lowlands, mountains, rocky terrain, and a river with waterfalls. Equally diverse is the architecture, which includes a water mill, windmill, and several churches. With today's energy consciousness, such mills are no longer viewed as picturesque and outmoded devices, but as intelligent uses of energy resources. The windmill shown here was used for grinding grain.[2] The small chapel in the foreground would have housed a statue or relic, which could be viewed when one knelt before the opening. Found throughout Europe from the Middle Ages on, wayside chapels were an important part of peasant life.

27a Rijckaert, *Landscape with Windmills*, 1628, panel, 23 x 26 cm. Present whereabouts unknown

The extremely warm tones of the painting's foreground contrast strongly with the cool tones of the distance. A transition occurs along the river at the lower right and includes the ecclesiastical complex in the middle-ground. Here the artist creates a sparkling effect through a skillful combination of pinks and blues, which are repeated in a subtle gradient across the sky.

This work appears to have been painted late in Rijckaert's career; its handling of figures and landscape elements has much in common with his *Landscape with Windmills* of 1628 (fig. 27a).[3] At this time, he was less attracted to the landscapes of Paul Bril, which he would have seen in Italy, and more influenced by artists back home like Joos de Momper and Jan Brueghel the Elder.

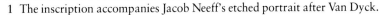

Verso: At the top in paint *Roland Xavary* (above *Saveria*) *162(0?)* and two signatures(?).

Provenance: Dealer, Julius Böhler, Munich, as by Joos de Momper and Jan Brueghel the Elder, 1953; Hon. Samuel Reber, Cologne; Mrs. Miles Reber.

1 The inscription accompanies Jacob Neeff's etched portrait after Van Dyck.

2 Although two arms of the windmill are partially cropped, the painting was not cut down at a later time, for there is original paint along the top edge of the panel.

3 This and three other signed and dated works are discussed by T.V. Frimmel, "Bilder von seltenen Meistern," *Hugo Helbing's Monatsberichte* 2: 384–85.

Jacques Ignatius de Roore *1686–1747*

28

Achilles with the Body of Hector, 1733
Oil on canvas, 37.6 x 42.2 cm

De Roore, the son of an Antwerp picture dealer, studied in both his home town and Brussels. He became a master in the Antwerp guild in 1707 and about 1720 moved to Holland, where he was active as both painter and art dealer.

The scene depicted here comes from Homer's account of the Trojan War (*Iliad* 22:395–515). The Greek hero Achilles had withdrawn from the war, but when his best friend, Patroclus, was killed by Hector, Achilles entered the battle and slew the Trojan in one-on-one combat. Instead of returning the body to the Trojans for a proper funeral, Achilles, in his anger, tied the body to the back of a chariot and dragged it in front of the walls of Troy in full view of Hector's parents and his wife, Andromache.

Only a few Dutch and Flemish artists have depicted the story of Hector and Achilles. Rubens incorporated it into a series of oil sketches representing the life of Achilles, painted about 1630 to 1632 as designs for tapestries.[1] He chose to portray the actual struggle between Hector and Achilles (fig. 28a), while hinting at succeeding events by including in the background the entrance to Troy and four white horses, doubtless the horses of Achilles's chariot. It was the gruesome scene of the dragging, however, that was focused on by most artists, as seen in a work attributed to the late-seventeenth-century Flemish painter Gérard de Lairesse (fig. 28b).

De Roore's painting is rather unusual in that it represents neither the struggle nor the dragging but the time in between. Dressed in armor specially made by Hephaestus and given to him by Thetis, Achilles stands triumphant over the dead Hector. The lifeless body with its mortal wound at the neck lies stripped of its armor, which appears in a pile at the left. A soldier with a knife standing over the dead Hector recalls Homer's account that "other Achaians hastened round to see Hector's fine body and comely face, and no one came who did not stab the body." In his left hand, Achilles holds what appears to be the thongs with which he will bind Hector's heels to the chariot being readied behind him. Farther back are the walls of Troy from which soldiers look down upon the scene.

28a Peter Paul Rubens, Flemish, 1577–1640, *The Death of Hector*, panel, 44 x 51.5 cm. Museum Boymans-van Beuningen, Rotterdam

28b Attributed to Gérard de Lairesse, Flemish, 1641–1711, *Achilles Drags the Body of Hector around the Walls of Troy*, canvas, 73 x 98 cm. Staatliche Kunst-sammlungen, Kassel

The painting exhibits the light palette and decorative style of the eighteenth century. The tall, slender proportions, graceful gestures, and ornate costumes all impart an air of elegance to the otherwise ghastly subject. The decorative effect is complemented by a brilliant display of brushwork. In many instances the artist used the butt end of his brush to draw directly into the wet paint, as seen in the horses, the pleated skirts of the men, and the signature and date at the lower right. The work is also an example of how eighteenth-century artists benefited from the fluid and spontaneous brushwork of Rubens, especially his oil sketches. De Roore was personally familiar with the sketches, having owned a large number of them.[2]

The sketch-like quality and size of De Roore's picture suggests that it was a modello or preparatory study for a larger work. At the time it was done, De Roore was living in Holland, where he was involved in painting large historical, mythological, and religious scenes to decorate the walls and ceilings of patrician homes in Amsterdam and The Hague.

This painting appears to be one of the works included in the artist's estate, which was sold in The Hague on 4 September 1747. The sale lists six paintings on the life of Achilles,[3] a series similar to the one that Rubens painted about a century earlier.[4] There is reason to believe that the six De Roore paintings were small-scale studies for larger works and that this is one of those studies.[5] Whereas the Rubens Achilles sketches were made as designs for tapestries, De Roore's were apparently part of an interior decoration project, since one of them is listed as a "ceiling" painting.[6] A specific architectural setting is also suggested in the painting exhibited here by the ledge in the immediate foreground, which runs the full width of the canvas. Such framing devices, a regular element in De Roore's decorative works, serve as a transition between the painted scene and the actual frame or molding. To add to the illusionistic effect, the artist frequently overlapped the painted molding with something from the scene itself, in this case a few branches of the small tree at the left.[7]

Unfortunately nothing is known about who might have commissioned De Roore to paint the cycle or whether it was ever carried out on a large scale. Many decorative series from this period are known to have been lost when the buildings themselves were destroyed, and often, as in this case, the modello or preparatory sketch is the only remaining record.

Signed lower right *J. De. Roore, I F,/1733*

Verso: Label inscribed *N395, Ec.flam./Roore/Jacque de/Lt. 38 L.40*. Inscribed on modern stretcher strip *"Achille fait liet le corps/mort de Hector."/Iliade d'Homère./By/Jacques de Roore/A.D. 1733.*

Provenance: De Roore estate sale, Hendrik Verheyden, The Hague, 4 September 1747, no. 147; sale, A & S. de Groot, The Hague, 20 March 1771, no. 100, bought by Schuller; Hermitage, Leningrad; sale, Leningrad, June 1854, no. 595; dealer, W. A. Martin & Brian Sewell, London, 1970–71; Hazlitt, Gooden & Fox Ltd., London; private collection.[8]

References: N. Wrangell, "L'Empereur Nicolas I et les arts," *Starye Gody* 7–9 (July–September 1913): 120, no. 595; *Allegemeines Lexikon der bildenden Künstler*, s.v. "De Roore," p. 577 (see n. 5 below).

Exhibition: Martin & Sewell, London, November 1970–January 1971, no. 12 (illus.).

1 See E. Haverkamp Begemann, *Corpus Rubenianum Ludwig Burchard*, vol. 10: *The Achilles Series* (New York: Phaidon, 1975), cat. no. 7, pp. 130–34; and J. S. Held, *The Oil Sketches of Peter Paul Rubens: A Critical Catalogue*, 2 vols. (Princeton: Princeton University Press, 1980), 1: 181–82, cat. nos. 126, 127.

2 The sale of De Roore's estate included many works by Rubens, seven of which were identified as sketches for the ceiling of the Jesuit Church of Antwerp (nos. 39–45). Among the other works by Rubens, at least five (nos. 54, 61, 62, 65, 72), although not identified as such, are also considered sketches; see Held, *Sketches*, nos. 176, 208, 306, 333, 343.

3 In addition to this painting (*Achilles by 't doode Lyk van den overwonnen Hector;* no. 147), the other works are: Achilles and Thetis (no. 144), Education of Achilles by Chiron (no. 145), Achilles and the Daughters of Lycomedes (no. 146), Death of Achilles (no. 148), Achilles among the Gods (no. 149).

4 Rubens's cycle does not include Achilles among the Gods, but does include three additional scenes: Wrath of Achilles, Briseis Returned to Achilles, and Thetis Receiving the Arms of Achilles from Hephaestus.

5 In the sale, the works are not specifically identified as sketches and unfortunately sizes are not given. Although some sketches in the 1747 sale are referred to as such, others are not, as in the case of several by Rubens (see n. 2). In any case, two of the paintings from this sale, The Education of Achilles (no. 145), and Achilles with the Body of Hector (no. 147), which were bought by a "De Groot," match the description of two works in the Anthoni de Groot estate sale held in The Hague on 20 March 1771, nos. 100 and 101, and in this sale the measurements are given; both paintings are 14 by 15 duims, which is approximately the same size as the work exhibited here. The De Groot paintings are identical in size and description to two that subsequently entered the Hermitage, Leningrad (the paintings are nos. 118 and 119 in E. Munich, "Catalogue raisonné des tableaux... Palais Impérial, de St. Petersbourg, commencé en 1773 et continue jusqu'en 1783," 1:341). The works were sold from the Hermitage collection in June 1854 under the direction of a Mr. Prevo (see Wrangell, *Starye Gody*, p. 120). It should be noted that the entry on De Roore in Thieme-Becker gives the *Starye Gody* reference, but incorrectly states that the two paintings were burned in 1832 instead of sold in 1854.

6 No. 149, *Achilles onder de Gooden, Plaffon.*

7 See, for example, his series of allegorical paintings completed in 1717 for the ceilings of the Council and Treasury Chambers of the Antwerp Town Hall. Both drapery and figures overlap a painted molding, the style of which relates to the actual molding.

8 See note 5.

Peter Paul Rubens *1577–1640*

29

The Beheading of Saint Paul
Oil on cradled panel, 38 x 23.3 cm

Throughout his career, Rubens made oil sketches in preparation for his commissions for large paintings. Long admired as works of art in themselves, these sketches have always been a favorite of collectors.[1] Rubens himself was very fond of his sketches and held on to a large number of them. Today they are appreciated by a much wider audience because of their freshness and spontaneity and the insights they provide into the master's creative process.[2]

This work is considered a preparatory sketch for Rubens's painting that once adorned the high altar in the church of the Augustinian priory of Rood Klooster near Brussels.[3] The large work, measuring almost fourteen feet high and installed in 1638, was destroyed by fire during the French invasion of 1695.[4]

Rubens's depiction of the preparations for Saint Paul's execution derive from the *Golden Legend*. On the way to his death, the saint met a pious woman named Plautilla, who gave him her kerchief to be used as a blindfold during his beheading. This act of mercy is the main focus of the sketch. The woman's compassion contrasts with the rough gesture of the executioner, who bares the martyr's shoulder with one hand and wields a sword in the other. Several Roman soldiers and some spectators frame the scene at the left and below, while overhead three angels bring a palm branch and laurel wreath, both symbols of the martyr's triumph over death.[5] The monument in the background is the pyramid of Caius Cestius, located near Rome's Ostia Gate, where Saint Paul's execution is supposed to have taken place.

The transparency of the sketch makes it easy to appreciate the various stages of its creation. First of all, the panel was covered with several layers of gesso and primed with a coarsely brushed film of brown paint. The priming is still clearly visible at the top. Rubens then began his composition by sketching with dark chalk; some of these lines can still be seen, especially below the angel with the laurel wreath (fig. 29a). Lines next to the wreath show that it originally was not in the center of the composition, but more to the right. With his chalk sketch as a guide, Rubens soon turned to paint, working with brown pigment for the medium to dark tones and lead white for the highlights. To this he eventually added color, using the primaries, red, blue, and yellow.

As Held has pointed out, Rubens concentrated on the largest and most prominent forms, gradually working his way toward the details.[6] The foreground figures would have probably been painted first, followed by those behind.

29a Detail of *The Beheading of Saint Paul*

Background elements, like the man on horseback, would have been inserted last. The same is true of the sky, which as one can see, was painted around the figures.

Provenance: Acquired by R. S. Holford in Florence from Mr. Wallace, 1847; Sir George Lindsay Holford, Dorchester House, London; sale, Christie's, London, 17–18 May 1928, no. 38; Knoedler, London, 1930; Scott & Fowles, N.Y., 1937; Joseph J. Kerrigan, N.Y.; Charles E. Roseman, Cleveland Heights, Ohio; Newhouse Galleries, N.Y.; Coll. Thomas M. Evans.

References: G. F. Waagen, *Treasures of Art in Great Britain,* 3 vols. (London: J. Murray, 1854), 2:200, as by Van Dyck *(The Beheading of a Saint);* M. Rooses, *L'Oeuvre de P. P. Rubens: Histoire et description de ses tableaux et dessins,* 5 vols. (Antwerp: J. Maes, 1886–92), 2: 333–35, no. 478; R. Oldenbourg, *P. P. Rubens: Des Meisters Gemälde* (Stuttgart: Deutsche Verlags-Anstalt, 1921), no. 418; R. Benson, ed., *The Holford Collection: Dorchester House,* 2 vols. (Oxford: Oxford University Press, 1927), 2: 16, no. 116, pl. 104; W. Gibson, "The Holford Collection," *Apollo* 7 (May 1928): 198–99; J. A. Goris and J. S. Held, *Rubens in America* (New York: Pantheon, 1947), p. 36, no. 67; E. Larsen, *P. P. Rubens, with a Complete Catalogue of His Works in America* (Antwerp: De Sikkel, 1952), p. 219, no. 92; F. van Molle, "Nieuwe nota's bij een verloren werk van P. P. Rubens," *Revue belge d'archéologie et d'histoire de l'art* 21 (1952): 127; L. Burchard and R.-A. d'Hulst, *Rubens Drawings,* 2 vols. (Brussels: Arcade, 1963), 1: 311; H. Vlieghe, "De Marteldood van H. Petrus, een olieverfschets door Gaspar de Crayer," *Bulletin Museum Boymans-van Beuningen* 17 (1966): 18, fig. 12; J. S. Held, "Jan van Boeckhorst as Draughtsman," *Bulletin des Musées Royaux des Beaux-Arts de Belgique* 16 (1967): 142; H. Vlieghe, *Corpus Rubenianum Ludwig Burchard,* vol. 8: *Saints,* 2 vols. (New York: Phaidon, 1973), 2: 133–34, 137, no. 137a; J. S. Held, *The Oil Sketches of Peter Paul Rubens: A Critical Catalogue,* 2 vols. (Princeton: Princeton University Press, 1980), 1: 582–83, no. 423, and 2: pls. 23, 412; G. Mulazzani, *Die grossen Meister der Malerei: Peter Paul Rubens,* 2 vols. (Berlin: Ullstein Kunstbuch, 1981), 2: nos. 503, 642 (same painting); G. Langemeyer, "Kunsthistorische Nachbemerkkungen zum Katalog der Werke des Johann Bockhorst," *Westfalen* 60 (1982): 194, fig. 13.

Exhibition: *Collectors' Opportunity,* Public Library, Winston-Salem, N.C., 22 April–3 May 1963, pp. 38–39 (illus.).

1 See p. 106.

2 For an appreciation of Rubens's oil sketches, see Held, *Sketches,* pp. 11–14.

3 Related to the oil sketch is a large chalk-and-wash drawing that Rubens may have had a hand in. For a discussion of this problematic drawing, see Vlieghe, *Saints,* 1: 136–37, and Held, *Sketches,* 1: 583.

4 At the time of the invasion, the painting was separated from its frame and moved into Brussels, where ironically it was destroyed. Judging from the frame, which still exists, it measured about 420 by 270 cm.

5 It was Saint Paul who compared the victorious Christian's crown to that of an athlete's, except for the fact that the former never fades (1 Cor. 9: 24–27).

6 See Held, *Sketches,* 1: 583.

Peeter Snijers 1681–1752

30

A Still Life of Fruit
Oil on canvas, 35.7 x 39.5 cm

30a Snijers, *Still Life of Fruit*, canvas, 36 x 39 cm. Private collection (photo: courtesy Galerie Robert Finck)

Peeter Snijers entered the Antwerp guild in 1707. From around 1720 to 1726 he was in England, where he painted mainly portraits. His usual subjects, however, were landscapes and still lifes of flowers and fruit. In 1741 he became one of the directors of the Antwerp Academy, which eventually replaced the Saint Luke's Guild. Also an active collector, Snijers acquired a large number of paintings by major artists of the preceding century.

Snijers's *Still Life of Fruit* is a contrast from the more decorative arrangements of his contemporaries. The artist made no attempt to idealize his subject, but instead shows numerous blemishes and damages on both fruit and leaves. The beauty lies in the vibrant colors, especially the reds and blues of the plums, which seem even more intense against the thinly painted, monochromatic background. Equally colorful are the insects, which include a tiger moth (*Arctia caja*) at the lower right, two blue bottle flies (*Calliphora vicina*) on one of the pears, and a fire cuckoo wasp (*Chrysis ignita*) on the apple.

This composition is virtually identical with another still life by Snijers, which is also signed (fig. 30a). The only major difference between the two is the rhinoceros beetle that appears at the lower left in the other work. The latter is one of a pair of paintings,[1] and it is possible that the work exhibited here was also once accompanied by a pendant.

Signed on ledge *Peeter:Snÿers*

Provenance: Mrs. R. MacMurray, MacLean, Va.; sale, Sotheby Parke Bernet, N.Y., 20 November 1980, no. 65 (illus.); private collection.

---

1 Both paintings are signed. They were last exhibited at the Galerie Robert Finck, Brussels, *Exposition de tableaux de mâitres du XVe au XVIIIe siècle*, 21 November – 14 December 1969, nos. 49, 50 (illus.).

Peeter : Snÿers

Jan Soens *1547-48—1611 or 1614*

31

The Meeting of Christ and Saint John the Baptist
Oil on canvas, 92.8 x 90.1 cm[1]

Born in 's Hertogenbosch, Soens trained at Antwerp under Gillis Mostaert. In 1573 he went to Rome, where he collaborated with Matthijs Bril on landscape frescoes in the Sala Ducale at the Vatican. The Dutch artist and writer Karel van Mander, who knew Soens in Rome, considered him one of the Netherlands's best landscape painters. Soens's talent was also recognized by Italian nobility; in 1575 he was called to Parma to be court painter to the Farnese Grand Dukes. There he spent the rest of his life.

Soens's success in Italy reflects the traditional Italian view that landscape was one of the major strengths of northern artists. This painting, which appears to date from Soens's years at Parma, combines both Netherlandish and Italian influences. The realistic and picturesque landscape with its progression of warm browns in the foreground to cool blues in the distance is characteristic of the North, while the elegant poses and subtle modeling of the main figures recall the work of Correggio, whose paintings at Parma had a strong influence on Soens.

The subject of this painting is rare in the history of art. It represents the moment when Christ asked Saint John to baptize Him. The actual baptism is recorded in all four gospels, but only Matthew (3:13–15) mentions the preceding request: "Then Jesus arrived at the Jordan from Galilee, and came to John to be baptized by him. John tried to dissuade him. 'Do you come to me?' he said; 'I need rather to be baptized by you.' Jesus replied, 'Let it be so for the present; we do well to conform in this way with all that God requires.'" Christ, identified by his halo, points toward the water, thus indicating His request; while Saint John, dressed in a tunic of animal skins, gestures to imply his own unworthiness. Meanwhile, three small angels prepare Christ by disrobing Him.

The baptism itself is the subject of another painting by Soens in which the setting is again a wooded landscape, with the Jordan treated as a mountain stream (fig. 31a). In both paintings, the main figures are placed close to the outside edge, a compositional device popular among Mannerist artists of the sixteenth century.

Scenes connected with Christ's baptism were a favorite among landscape artists because of the opportunities they provided for depicting the natural surroundings of the event. This is particularly evident in *The Meeting of Christ and Saint John*, in which numerous picturesque details help to carry the viewer through the landscape. In the far distance is a castle-like structure, and in the middle-ground, a bridge and some domestic buildings. On the

114

31a Soens, *Baptism of Christ*, canvas.
Museo di Capodimonte, Naples

bridge and elsewhere are figures whose sketchy quality contrasts with the
more solid rendering of those in the foreground. This more spontaneous treatment of background elements can be seen in a detail of the two men herding
animals along a path at the right (fig. 31b).

31b Detail of *The Meeting of Christ and Saint John the Baptist*

Provenance: Sale, Christie's, London, 10 December 1982, no. 1 *(Ecce Agnus Dei;* illus.); private collection.

1 This measurement includes part of the tacking edge at the top (1.5 cm) and bottom (2 cm), which was used to extend the composition. These strips, not part of the original design, are now concealed by the frame.

Joris van Son *1623–1667*

32

Still Life, 1658

Oil on canvas, 55.6 x 45.9 cm[1]

Joris van Son was a still-life specialist whose paintings almost always include fruit.[2] This work is no exception with its extremely colorful display of seven different varieties. Van Son's mouth-watering image shows several of the fruits already sliced and ready to be eaten, as well as a succulent oyster, an inviting loaf of bread, some walnuts, and a Lamberts nut at the lower right. As tempting as Van Son's still life is today, it must have been even more so in the seventeenth century, since most of the fruits depicted were not native to the Netherlands, but would have been imported.

Van Son's still life also includes wine in two kinds of glasses: one, a *Berke-meier* glass, rests on a wooden box, while the other, a *Roemer,* is supported by an elegant gold-and-silver glass holder known as a *bekerschroef.* This device was used to turn a simple glass into an elegant vessel by providing a stem and base. Judging from paintings, *bekerschroefs* were quite common in the seventeenth century, though the number of surviving originals is very small.[3] The gilded, upper portion of this one is decorated with mannerist designs, while the stem consists of a putto holding what may be a flame or piece of coral. Van Son must have been fond of this particular holder, for he used it in at least five other still lifes.[4] In several of the paintings, the lower part of the *bekerschroef* is more visible and shows the cupid seated on a dolphin (fig. 32a). Here, in addition to the glass, it supports a piece of grapevine whose arched form frames the middle portion of the painting and accentuates the overall pyramid design.

It is not known with whom Van Son studied, but he was greatly influenced by Jan Davidsz. de Heem, one of Antwerp's finest still-life painters who moved there from Holland in 1636. Van Son and Jan Davidsz.'s son, Cornelis, were perhaps the two best followers of the elder De Heem. It is interesting to compare this work with one of Cornelis de Heem's somewhat similar fruit still lifes painted about the same time (cat. no. 17). Both artists set their arrangements against a dark background on a stone ledge partially covered by drapery. The dramatic lighting calls attention to the foremost objects,

I.VAN.SON.F
1658

32a Van Son, *Fruit Still Life with Boiled Lobster,* panel, 56.2 x 87.1 cm. Staatliche Kunsthalle, Karlsruhe, West Germany

some of which, including the pewter plate, seem to project into the viewer's own space. In Van Son's painting the lighting is softer and results in a greater differentiation between the textures of the various objects.

Van Son adds to the illusionism of this work by including numerous droplets of water. Another illusionistic device, which appears in many of his still lifes, is the tiny piece of straw that leans against one of the apricots, casting a shadow on it and the box (fig. 32b).[5] Such *trompe l'oeil* details would have delighted the seventeenth-century collector as much as they do a collector today.

32b Detail of *Still Life*

Signed on ledge *I.VAN.SON.F/1658*

Provenance: Sale, Ader-Picard-Tajan, Hôtel Drouot, Paris, 29 April 1982, no. 45 (illus.); Kunsthandel P. de Boer, Amsterdam, 1982; private collection.

Exhibition: *Fine Arts of the Netherlands*, The Waldorf-Astoria Hotel, N.Y., 20–28 November 1982.

1 This measurement includes a strip of canvas at the top that is 3.2 cm wide and was originally the tacking edge; it was later used to extend the composition and is now concealed by the frame.

2 Studies on Van Son include E. Greindl, *Les Peintres flamands de nature morte au XVIIe siècle* (Brussels: Elsevier, 1956), pp. 111–13, 187–89; A.P. de Mirimonde, "Joris et Jan van Son dans les musées de province," *La Revue des arts* 10 (1960): 7–18; S. Segal, "Joris van Son," in *A Selection of Dutch and Flemish Seventeenth-Century Paintings* (New York: Hoogsteder-Naumann, 1983), pp. 76–81.

3 For one of the few surviving examples, see A.L. den Blaauwen, *Dutch Silver 1580–1830*, exh. cat. (Amsterdam: Rijksmuseum, 1979), pp. 30–31, no. 14.

4 One dated 1651 and another 1658, the same year as this work. The 1651 painting, *A Vanitas Still Life* (canvas, 77 x 110.5 cm), was sold by Sotheby's, London, on 12 July 1978, no. 222 (illus.). The 1658 painting (canvas, 74 x 58 cm, signed), last recorded in a private collection in Brussels, is illustrated in Greindl, *Les Peintres*, fig. 73. Other Van Son still lifes in which the same *bekerschroef* appears include: *Fruit Still Life with Boiled Lobster*, panel, 56.2 x 87.1 cm, signed, Staatliche Kunsthalle, Karlsruhe, no. 219; *Still Life*, canvas, 81 x 106 cm, signed, sale, Bukowski, Stockholm, 30 October 1979, no. 452 (illus.); *Vanitas Still Life*, canvas, 52.5 x 68 cm, signed, P. de Boer, Amsterdam, 1983.

5 For other illustrations of this detail, see Greindl, *Les Peintres*, fig. 72, and S. Segal, "Joris van Son," p. 76.

David Teniers the Younger 1610–1690

33

A Picture Gallery
Oil on canvas, 60 x 75.5 cm

A Picture Gallery, painted around 1670, represents the kind of collection that became popular in Antwerp around the middle of the seventeenth century.[1] Focusing on the fine arts—paintings, sculpture, prints, and drawings—these collections were a marked contrast to the assemblages of art and curiosities that filled the earlier *Wunderkammern* (see cat. no. 21).

The proud and well-dressed collector sits at a table surrounded by his treasures. He is unidentified and probably not meant to represent a specific person. The status of the more plainly dressed man holding a wax seal is uncertain. He may be another collector, a dealer, or possibly someone charged with looking after the younger man's collection. On the table before them are drawings, sculpture, medals, and additional seals. The collection is Teniers's own invention, although it is based on one that was well known to him and many of the paintings can be identified. Almost all the pictures on the back wall belonged to Archduke Leopold Wilhelm, former governor general of the Southern Netherlands,[2] who by this time had moved with his collection from Brussels to Vienna.

Teniers was court painter to the archduke during the latter's stay in the Netherlands (1647–56) and also served as his curator. He painted numerous interior views of the collection (see Introduction) and also made small-scale copies of the archduke's Italian paintings for the use of engravers who recorded the collection in *Theatrum Pictorum* published in 1660.[3] In *A Picture Gallery,* Teniers has taken liberties with some of the archduke's paintings, adjusting size and content to fit the particular arrangement. Several of the images are reversed, suggesting that Teniers probably referred to the engravings.

The paintings in *A Picture Gallery* that can be connected with Leopold Wilhelm are all Italian. Confined to the back wall, they are hung literally from floor to ceiling and one even overlaps another. Almost all of the works on the other two walls and in the foreground are Flemish. Some of these may also have belonged to Leopold Wilhelm, who owned even more northern European paintings than Italian.[4] Still, it was the Italian paintings that were the favorite of the archduke and which are shown in greatest number in Teniers's many depictions of his collection. Here, by contrast, greater prominence is

D · TENIERS · FEC

given to the work of Teniers's fellow countrymen. Most of the more recent Flemish paintings are set off even further by gold frames, which by the second half of the seventeenth century were favored over simple, black moldings.

The painting of the Madonna and Child on the floor in front of the easel is the only sixteenth-century Flemish work (fig. 33a). There are a number of versions of this composition, all of which are thought to derive from a lost painting by Jan Gossaert.[5] The one in the museum at Liège, which is attributed to Pieter Coecke van Aelst (fig. 33b), is the most similar to the painting in *A Picture Gallery,* which may represent the Gossaert original.

The most prominent position—on the easel—is given to a peasant scene that is, without question, a work by Teniers (fig. 33a). The composition cannot be linked with any surviving original and probably was painted specifically for the imaginary gallery.[6] Other Flemish paintings are so detailed, attributions can be made for them as well. The winter landscape, for example, appears to be by Joos de Momper.[7]

Although specific enough to be associated with other artists (fig. 33c), all of the paintings in *A Picture Gallery* exhibit the light, delicate touch characteristic of Teniers's mature style. Nowhere is this more apparent than in the Gossaert, the original of which would have had a smoother, enamel-like surface (see cat. no. 14).

The monkey and dog, which occupy a main position in the foreground, may seem out of place in a gallery; however, the monkey symbolizes the art of painting and sculpture. Because the artist's skill was regarded as imitative, it was linked with the animal known for its mimicry. *Ars simia naturae,* "art is the ape of nature," was a popular saying and the inspiration for many seventeenth-century Flemish paintings that humorously showed the monkey in the role of the artist.[8] Teniers himself painted several examples of this parody, such as the one in the Prado (fig. 33d). Another animal associated with mimicry is the parrot, which may explain the one perched on the open window at the upper left.

Wearing a red-and-yellow costume of a fool and surrounded by artistic treasures,[9] the monkey devotes all his attention to the apple in his hand. He may be considered a fool for ignoring the works of art around him. On the other hand, his fascination with the apple may be a parody of the collector's fascination with his *objets d'art.*

33a Detail of *A Picture Gallery*

33b Pieter Coecke van Aelst, Flemish, 1502–1550, *Virgin Reading,* panel, 44.5 x 34.5 cm. Musée Archéologique Curtius, Liège (photo: A.C.L., Brussels)

33c Paintings depicted in *A Picture Gallery*
1. Landscape; 2. Lot and His Daughters;
3. Winter Landscape, Joos de Momper;
4. Grotto Landscape; 5. Moonlight Landscape; 6. Portrait of a Man; 7. *Portrait of
the Doge Nicolas da Ponte,* Tintoretto
(Kunsthistorisches Museum, Vienna);
8. *Portrait of a White Bearded Man,* Tintoretto (Kunsthistorisches Museum, Vienna);
9. *Portrait of a Man,* Tintoretto; 10. Saint
or Prophet; 11. *The Blind Leading the
Blind,* Domenico Fetti (Gemäldegalerie,
Dresden); 12. Landscape with Saint
Anthony(?); 13. *Landscape with Shepherd,*
Jacopo Bassano; 14. *Marcus Curius Denta-
tus,* Schiavone (Kunsthistorisches Museum,
Vienna); 15. *Saint Jerome,* Dosso Dossi
(Kunsthistorisches Museum, Vienna);
16. Elijah Visited by an Angel; 17. Portrait
of a Woman; 18. Peasants Merrymaking,
David Teniers the Younger; 19. Portrait of
a Doge; 20. *A Warrior,* Pietro della Vecchia
(Kunsthistorisches Museum, Vienna;
21. *Madonna and Child,* Jan Gossaert;
22. Portrait of a Man in a Black Skull Cap;
23. Battle Scene; 24. Harbor Scene, Bona-
ventura Peeters(?)

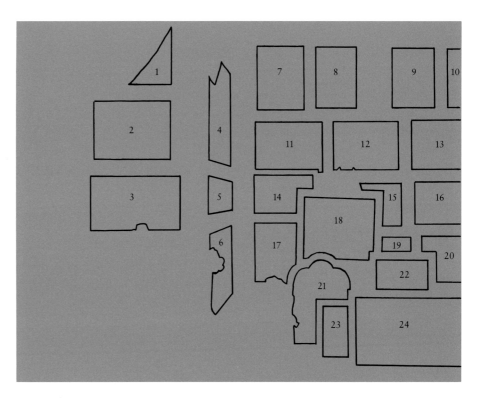

33d Teniers, *The Monkey Painter,* canvas,
24 x 32 cm. Prado, Madrid

Signed lower right *D • TENIERS • FEC*

Provenance: Lord Courtenay, 1816; The Hon. General Phipps, M.P., 1821; The Hon. Edmund Phipps, Esq., 1847; sale, Christie's, London, 25 June 1859, no. 60 *(Interior of the Picture Gallery of the Archduke Leopold)*; Edmond Rothschild; Noortman, Maastricht, May 1982, no. 8 (illus.); Coll. Saul Steinberg.

References: *An Account of All the Pictures Exhibited in the Rooms of the British Institution from 1813 to 1823* (London: Priestley and Weale, 1924), p. 200, no. 26 *(Interior of the Emperor Leopold's Gallery)*; J. Smith, *A Catalogue Raisonné of the Works of the Most Eminent Dutch, Flemish and French Painters,* 9 vols. (London: Smith and Son, 1829–42), 3:379, no. 455; G. F. Waagen, *Treasures of Art in Great Britain,* 3 vols. (London: John Murray, 1854), 2:228, no. 1.

Exhibitions: British Institution, London, 1821, no. 39; British Institution, London, 1847, no. 39 *(The Leopold Gallery).*

---

1 A copy of *A Picture Gallery* (canvas, 63.5 x 80 cm), formerly in the collection of Dr. C.J.K. van Aalst, Hoevelaken, The Netherlands, was sold by Christie's, London, 1 April 1960, no. 50. The copy suggests that the original painting has been trimmed, especially at the top and sides. The copy, for example, includes the entire frame on the seascape at the lower right.

2 Not surprisingly, *A Picture Gallery* has often been referred to as a view of Leopold Wilhelm's gallery; see provenance.

3 The *Theatrum Pictorum,* also known as the "Teniers Gallery," illustrates 244 of the archduke's Italian paintings. See S. Speth-Holterhoff, *Les Peintres flamands de cabinets d'amateurs au XVIIe siècle* (Brussels: Elsevier, 1957), pp. 127–60, and K. Schütz, "David Teniers der Jüngere als Kopist in Dienst Erzherzog Leopold Wilhelms," in *Original-Kopie-Replik-Paraphrase,* exh. cat. (Vienna: Akademie der bildenden Künste, 1980), pp. 21–33.

4 When he left the Netherlands, Leopold Wilhelm owned 517 Italian paintings and 880 Flemish, Dutch, and German. The four pieces of sculpture in *A Picture Gallery* and the dolphin-legged table on which they stand all appear in other paintings by Teniers. See, for example, fig. 33d and Teniers's art gallery painting in Schleissheim Gemäldegalerie.

5 There are at least eight variants of this work, two of which are given to Pieter Coecke van Aelst. See G. Marlier, *La Renaissance flamande: Pierre Coeck d'Alost* (Brussels: Robert Finck, 1966), pp. 242–44.

6 The painting recalls several of Teniers's peasant merrymaking scenes, for example, one dated 1675, sold by Christie's, London, 18 April 1980, no. 12, and another in a private Swiss collection that Margret Klinge dates about 1660 *(Adriaen Brouwer, David Teniers the Younger,* exh. cat. [New York: Noortman & Brod, 1982], no. 47 [illus.]). See the entry on Van Kessel (cat. no. 21) for another example of an artist who composed "paintings" for his paintings.

7 The closest known original is in the De Boer Collection, Amsterdam; see *Collectie Stichting P. en N. de Boer, Amsterdam,* exh. cat. (Laren: Singer Museum, 1966), no. 117, fig. 51. Even closer in composition is a drawing in the Lugt Collection, Paris, which has been connected with the De Boer painting and others. See *Flemish Drawings of the Seventeenth Century from the Collection of Frits Lugt, Institut Néerlandais, Paris,* exh. cat. (Paris: Institut Néerlandais, 1972), no. 55, pl. 16.

8 See H. W. Janson, *Apes and Ape Lore in the Middle Ages and the Renaissance* (London: Warburg Institute, 1952), esp. pp. 287–325.

9 A monkey wearing a fool's costume of the same colors appears in Cornelis de Baellieur's gallery interior dated 1637 (Louvre, M. I. 699).

Unidentified Artist *early 16th century*

34

Landscape with Saint Anthony
Oil on panel, 22.5 x 14.9 cm (panel)

Reproduced here in its actual size, this small panel with its sweeping view of nature is a good example of the type of landscape that Flemish artists developed in the early sixteenth century. Although artists of the preceding century included similar scenes in the backgrounds of their paintings, it was now, for the first time, that landscape became an acceptable primary subject for a work of art. The earliest known landscape specialist was the Antwerp artist Joachim Patinir; his meticulously rendered panoramic views were a major influence in establishing landscape as an independent genre.

This painting has much in common with a group of landscapes once attributed to Patinir, but now ascribed to an unknown artist who has been given the name Master of the (Female) Half-Lengths.[1] Active during the second quarter of the sixteenth century, the Half-Lengths Master painted both figural subjects—as his name implies—and landscapes. His landscapes are of high quality. Extremely close in style to those of Patinir, they exhibit an even greater attention to naturalistic detail and a more refined type of figure. Using thinner glazes than Patinir, the Master achieves a wider range of greens in the middle distance, which tend to carry over more into the far distance. The clouds in his paintings, in contrast to the large, cumulus type usually found in Patinir's, are generally more stratified, repeating the horizontal lines of the land. The Half-Lengths Master also features a greater variety of animals, which often appear in pairs.

This landscape compares best with works thought to have been painted at the beginning of the Half-Lengths Master's career, in the early 1520s, when he may have been working in Patinir's studio.[2] The small panel shows clearly a debt to Patinir and, at the same time, an increase in naturalistic detail, which foreshadows future developments in landscape painting.

In the early sixteenth century there were strong relationships between landscape painting and mapmaking, an art that was also developing in Antwerp at this time. Here, as on a map, one can wander from river to ocean, from village to town, and from valley to mountain. The topographical image is a series of vignettes, each separated, yet also linked, by the wooded areas in between. In the middle-ground, for example, lies a medieval city, with its towers, surrounding walls, and entry gate. Beyond the city, a bridge spans an estuary and several tall structures rise along the shore. The perspective varies throughout: the land and water are seen from above, while vertical elements, like buildings, trees, and mountains, are at eye level.

Absorbed in reading the scriptures, Saint Anthony (A.D. ca. 251–350) ignores the worldly panorama spread out behind him. The son of wealthy Egyptian parents, he decided at a young age to distribute his property among the poor and retire into the desert to live the life of a hermit. Considered the father of monasticism, he appears here in a monk's cloak and cowl. The *tau*, or T-shaped cross, on the saint's left shoulder is an ancient Egyptian symbol long associated with him. The pig, an animal bred by the Antonine monks during the Middle Ages, is another of Saint Anthony's attributes; pig lard was believed to be a cure for ergotism, a fungus disease formerly known as Saint Anthony's fire. The rock and spring to the left of the saint are also significant: common motifs in sixteenth-century religious landscapes, they symbolize Christ and the gospel and here refer specifically to the spirituality of the hermit-saint.[3]

34a Detail of *Landscape with Saint Anthony*

The landscape includes several other figures who wear the black robe of the Antonine order. Off to the left, just in front of the first group of trees, a pair of monks appear to be attending a third monk who lies on the ground between them. This scene may refer to Saint Anthony's rescue by one of his brothers following an attack by devilish monsters.[4] Two more monks can be seen farther back, next to the stream. One fishes while the other calls to him from across the water (fig. 34a). A third figure appears next to the mill's water wheel, and a fourth leads a donkey carrying a pack. Even farther in the distance, one barely discernible figure heads toward the architectural complex at the upper left. This group of buildings, which includes a large church, appears to be the monastery.

Landscape with Saint Anthony is not only a microcosm of topography and architecture, but also a sampler of flora and fauna. Along the bottom edge are several plantains (*Plantago maior*), a common plant, which because of its ability to be trodden upon and remain undamaged was associated with humility, an appropriate attribute for Saint Anthony. Several other plants in the foreground may also have religious meaning.[5] The creeping thistle (*Cirsium arvense*) in front of the saint is traditionally associated with sin, earthly sorrow, or evil (Genesis 3:18). The long-stemmed plant to the right of the pig is a mullein or Aaron's Rod (*Verbascum thapsus*) whose bright yellow flowers were a symbol of Christ, the Light of the World. Finally, the large plant to the left of the saint, a mallow (*Malva sylvestris*), was associated with salvation because of its medicinal properties.

Besides the pig and donkey, the domestic animals include numerous sheep and a cow, all in the background (fig. 34a). At the lower left are a variety of birds: a pair of swans, two mallards, a stork, a spoonbill, and, perched on the large rock, a magpie. In back of Saint Anthony, a rabbit leaps out from behind a tree. Two small lizards, which almost go unnoticed, flank one of the plantains

34b Detail of *Landscape with Saint Anthony*

at the bottom (fig. 34b). These reptiles may refer to the temptations of Saint Anthony either directly or indirectly, since the lizard was both a symbol of evil and a protector against it.[6]

Provenance: Mrs. Gustav D. Klimann.

1 The Master of the Half-Lengths's landscape development and oeuvre were first extensively established by Robert A. Koch, *Joachim Patinir* (Princeton: Princeton University Press, 1968), pp. 56–65. Koch devotes a separate chapter to the Master in which he reattributes to him works wrongly ascribed to Patinir. I am grateful to Professor Koch for his comments on *Landscape with Saint Anthony*.

2 It should be compared with the two landscapes with Saint Jerome (Kansas City and Zurich; Koch, *Patinir*, cat. nos. M.H.-L. 8 and 9).

3 A. P. de Mirimonde, "Le Symbolisme du rocher et de la source chez Joos van Clève, Dirck Bouts, Memling, Patenier, C. van den Broeck (?), Sustris et Paul Bril," *Jaarboek Koninklijk Museum voor Schone Kunsten, Antwerpen*, 1974, pp. 73–100.

4 G. Ryan and H. Ripperger, trans., *Legend Aurea of Jacobus de Voragine* (New York: Longman, Green and Co., 1948), p. 100. After a second attack by demons, Saint Anthony was addressed by Christ. This account is illustrated in the background of Patinir's *Temptation of Saint Anthony* in the Prado (Koch, *Patinir*, no. 17).

5 In 15th-century Flemish painting, plants almost always have specific religious meanings. In later paintings, however, it is not always clear if they are symbolic or simply naturalistic detail.

6 On the symbolism of the lizard, see S. Segal, "The Flower Pieces of Roelandt Savery," *Leids kunsthistorisch jaarboek*, 1982, p. 324.

131

Otto van Veen 1556–1629

35

The Adoration of the Shepherds
Oil on copper, 87.6 x 73.3 cm

Best known today as one of the teachers of Rubens, Otto van Veen led a life similar to that of his most famous pupil. Born into a family of some distinction, he studied in the Netherlands and Italy, traveled rather extensively, and spent most of his years in Antwerp, where he had a large studio and painted for the court. A distinguished and scholarly artist, Van Veen strongly influenced Rubens, who studied with him from 1596 to 1598 and then assisted him for two more years before leaving for Italy.

The Adoration of the Shepherds, which appears to date just after 1600, exhibits the mild classicism characteristic of figure painting in Antwerp during the first decade of the seventeenth century. Like many of his contemporaries, Van Veen arrived at this style after gradually abandoning Mannerism. To appreciate the change, one should compare this painting to another Nativity by him completed shortly before 1600 (fig. 35a). In the earlier work the figures are restless and contorted and appear to float across the picture plane, whereas in the later painting they are much more solid and relate more clearly to each other. Although both works incorporate dramatic lighting, in the earlier painting it is used for decorative and ambiguous effects, while here it serves to model the figures and organize them into a coherent design.

With its dense, solidly constructed forms and figures that appear frozen in space, Van Veen's *Adoration* is somewhat static. The rigid, formal design is relieved by only a few small details, like the angels holding hands and the shepherd at the lower left, who smiles at the viewer while caressing the woman next to him. This kind of stiff, Flemish classicism was soon to be transformed by Rubens into the much more painterly and spirited art of the Baroque.

In Van Veen's earlier painting, the angel's announcement to the shepherds, inscribed on a banderole, is combined with the Nativity scene in the foreground. Here the announcement takes place on a distant hillside, where additional shepherds watch over their flocks (fig. 35b).

The Adoration of the Shepherds is closely related to another Nativity by Van Veen in the Gemäldegalerie, Schleissheim (fig. 35c), which is part of a series of fifteen paintings on the life of the Virgin.[1] The Schleissheim painting, a much smaller work, includes many similar figures and animals. The shepherd kneeling at the right, for example, is virtually identical.[2] And in both, Van Veen shows the shepherds presenting the Christ Child with their humble gifts: apples, eggs, birds, and a lamb. The apples probably refer to Christ as the new Adam, and the bound lamb to His future sacrifice.

35a Van Veen, *Nativity,* panel, 230.5 x 204.5 cm. Maagdenhuis, Antwerp (photo: A.C.L., Brussels)

35b Detail of *The Adoration of the Shepherds*

35c Van Veen, *Nativity*, copper, 23.5 x 32 cm. Gemäldegalerie, Schleissheim, West Germany

The Adoration of the Shepherds is painted on an unusually large and thick piece of copper. A popular painting support among Flemish artists during the seventeenth century, copper was valued for its fine surface and was, for the most part, used for smaller, highly detailed works. Punched into the back of this panel is the mark of the Antwerp coppersmith Pieter Stas, which consists of his initials inside a heart-shaped design. The mark appears twice, along with two hands, symbols of the Antwerp guild (fig. 35d).[3]

35d Mark of the coppersmith Pieter Stas

Verso: Marks of Antwerp coppersmith Pieter Stas (height of hand 5 cm; height of monogram .8 cm).

Provenance: Sale, Sotheby's, London, 8 April 1970, no. 40, bought by Kyrle Fletcher; Central Picture Galleries, N.Y.; private collection.

1 The paintings are all the same size, 23.5 by 32 cm, and on copper.

2 In the smaller work, the shepherd kneels against a mound of earth, which is missing in the larger painting, making his pose somewhat uncertain.

3 See p. 49, n.3. Some of Stas's copper panels also include a date. Although this one does not, one can assume it was made before 1608, for on panels of that year and later, Stas used a more elaborate mark that spells out his name.

Nicolas van Veerendael 1640–1691

36

Still Life with Flowers, 1689
Oil on canvas, 80.5 x 62.5 cm

36a Van Veerendael, *Flowers and Fruit*, 1689, canvas, 81 x 62 cm. Evansville Museum of Arts and Science, Indiana

This still life, one of Van Veerendael's last dated works, exhibits the broad, decorative style of late-seventeenth-century floral painting. It is a pendant to another still life by the artist now in the Evansville Museum (fig. 36a). In both works the flowers weave in and out of a strong, foreground light to create an overall decorative pattern. The two large terra-cotta urns are used not so much as containers for the flowers as forms on which to drape them. In effect, both paintings are a cross between the traditional still life and the floral garland, a typical Flemish genre that also appears in Van Veerendael's oeuvre.

A native of Antwerp, Van Veerendael was one of the town's leading flower painters during the second half of the seventeenth century. His early works, which are generally on a smaller scale, are more refined and exhibit a greater use of glazes. This later, more ambitious composition is characterized by a much warmer palette, with the cool tones restricted to a few blue flowers.

Van Veerendael was noted for the variety of flowers he included in a single work.[1] In this painting there are over thirty species, all identifiable except for the white blossom at the lower left, which may be an invention of the artist or a plant no longer cultivated.[2] Some blossoms, such as the Rose of Sharon, appear in almost all of his floral still lifes.

Signed and dated lower left *N.V. Veerendael 1689*

Provenance: Galerie Robert Finck, Brussels, 1967, with pendant; American dealer; sale, Christie's, N.Y., 11 January 1979, no. 69, with pendant (illus.); private collection.

Reference: *A Selection of Dutch and Flemish Seventeenth-Century Paintings* (New York: Hoogsteder-Naumann, 1983), p. 92, fig. 4.

Exhibitions: *Mostra mercato internazionale dell'antiquariato*, Palazzo Strozzi, Florence, 22 September–22 October 1967, no. 50, with pendant (illus.); *Exposition de tableaux de mâitres du XVᵉ au XIXᵉ siècle*, Galerie Robert Finck, Brussels, 24 November–17 December 1967, no. 39, with pendant (illus.).

1 See Sam Segal's entry in *Dutch and Flemish Paintings*, pp. 87–93.

2 I am grateful to Sam Segal for identifying the flowers in the two 1889 pendants.

Cornelis de Vos *ca. 1584–1651*

37

Portrait of a Gentleman
Oil on cradled panel, 104 x 73.5 cm

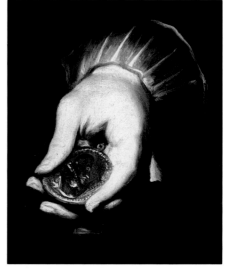

37a Detail of *Portrait of a Gentleman*

One of Antwerp's most successful portrait painters, Cornelis de Vos was influenced by both Rubens and Van Dyck. In this portrait, which dates from around 1620, De Vos offers an image of reserved dignity that would have appealed to Antwerp's wealthy middle class.

Framed by an elaborate collar, the man's face, with its creamy-white complexion set off by dark, penetrating eyes, is fully illuminated and sensitively modeled. The brilliant red drapery—which, like the classical column, was by this time standard embellishment in fashionable Flemish portraiture—adds color to the rather austere image. De Vos also includes part of a table covered with a Turkish carpet on which there are some rings, coins, and a container for the medal held by the unknown gentleman. On the medal is another portrait, a profile of a man whose costume dates from the second half of the sixteenth century (fig. 37a). By displaying the medal, the gentleman may be identifying himself as a collector, or he may be indicating a special relationship between him and the man depicted on the medal, perhaps an ancestor.

The three-quarter-length portrait was a favorite format of De Vos's, who often used it for pendant portraits of married couples—the man on the left, the woman on the right.[1] Whether or not this portrait had a pendant is unknown.

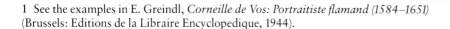

Provenance: Mortimer Brandt; sale, Parke-Bernet, N.Y., 3 November 1954, no. 38 (*Portrait of a Collector;* illus.); Peter L. Durk; sale, Sotheby Parke-Bernet, N.Y., 22–23 January 1976, no. 230; private collection; sale, Sotheby Parke-Bernet, N.Y., 21 January 1982, no. 99 (illus.); private collection.

1 See the examples in E. Greindl, *Corneille de Vos: Portraitiste flamand (1584–1651)* (Brussels: Editions de la Libraire Encyclopedique, 1944).

Paul de Vos ca. 1596–1678
Theodor van Thulden 1606–1669

38

The Hunt of Diana
Oil on canvas, 157 x 200.5 cm

In this large, colorful, action-packed hunting scene, one can almost hear the cacophonous barking of the dogs chasing the two helpless deer. Like darts across the canvas, the dogs' long, sleek bodies create a tremendous sweep interrupted only by the backward glance of the frightened stag. Adding to the drama are the three gracefully posed figures of Diana and two companions.[1]

The animals in this painting are by Paul de Vos and the figures by Theodor van Thulden. The landscape may be the work of a third artist, Jan Wildens, who was a relative of De Vos and often collaborated with him. De Vos, who was the younger brother of the portrait and figure painter Cornelis (cat. no. 37), was a specialist in painting animals. In his numerous hunting scenes, strong baroque rhythms convey the excitement of the event. Here the drama is enhanced by the variety of colors and patterns of a dozen different dogs who emerge from all sides. Several of them, like one of the figures, are cut off by the edge of the composition, thus carrying the movement beyond the picture plane.

In the Albertina, Vienna, is a watercolor of three of the dogs that may have been done in preparation for the painting (fig. 38a). Considering its high degree of finish, however, as well as its totally different landscape, the work may have been made for its own sake after the painting. Until it was recently connected with this composition, the watercolor, like so many of De Vos's works, was misattributed to his brother-in-law, Frans Snyders, the best known of the Flemish animal painters.[2]

Hunting scenes were a popular Flemish genre. A favorite among private collectors both in Flanders and abroad, they were often used to decorate princely residences and hunting lodges. Next to Rubens, De Vos was probably the most successful painter to convey the energy and movement of the hunt, whether it be a mythological one, as here, or a contemporary event.

Van Thulden's three figures show the strong influence Rubens had on him, particularly in his early work. The fluid brushwork and overall blond tonality is characteristic of Van Thulden at this time. Most Rubensian is the woman with the bow, who appears to have missed with the arrow she has just shot. Her right arm, still held gracefully in the air, casts a pleasing shadow across her face. Her left, with the bow, is echoed by the arm with which Diana rather unconvincingly holds her spear. Clearly Van Thulden is more interested in the lyrical poses of his figures than their hunting expertise. De Vos takes a similar

38a De Vos, *Three Staghounds*, watercolor, 34 x 48 cm. Graphische Sammlung Albertina, Vienna

38b Peter Paul Rubens, Flemish, 1577–1640, *The Hunt of Diana,* panel, 27.8 x 57.7 cm. Coll. Maj. Gen. Sir Harold Wernher, Luton Hoo, England

approach. His two deer, for example, with their virtually identical poses, appear somewhat like animals on a carousel.

It may have been in the late 1630s, when both De Vos and Van Thulden were assisting Rubens on some of his large painting commissions, that the two younger artists joined forces to produce the work exhibited here.[3] Around this time Rubens himself painted several versions of the theme. A comparison of one of his sketches with this painting reveals the decorative quality of the latter (fig. 38b).[4] Both works convey drama, but only in Rubens's sketch are the actions of the figures and animals convincing. In the painting by De Vos and Van Thulden, it is not the realism that counts, but the graceful, theatrical effects.

Provenance: Sale, Galerie Fiévez, 30 March 1936, no. 53, as by Rubens and Snyders (illus.); sale, Van Herck, 25 November 1975, no. 180, as by Van Thulden and De Vos (illus.); private collection, Antwerp; P & D Colnaghi, N.Y., 1983; Coll. Daniel Varsano; private collection.

1 According to Arnout Balis, there are at least six copies of this work. The best was sold in Paris, Galliéra, 16 June 1967, no. 208. Another version was sold at Christie's, London, 13 April 1973, no. 92 (as by Rubens and P. de Vos).

2 I am grateful to Bob Haboldt for bringing this drawing to my attention. For the Snyders attribution, see C.R. Bordley, *Rubens ou Snyders?* (Paris: Le Nef, 1955), fig. 38 (reversed).

3 It was shortly after this time, around 1643, that Van Thulden left Antwerp to live in the town of his birth, 's Hertogenbosch.

4 Rubens painted at least three sketches of this subject (J.S. Held, *The Oil Sketches of Peter Paul Rubens: A Critical Catalogue*, 2 vols. [Princeton: Princeton University Press, 1980], nos. 186, 223, 237). The one illustrated here was done in connection with his decorations for King Philip IV's hunting lodge near Madrid, the Torre de la Parada, a project in which both De Vos and Van Thulden assisted. See S.L. Alpers, *Corpus Rubenianum Ludwig Burchard*, vol. 9: *The Decoration of the Torre de la Parada* (New York: Phaidon, 1971), pp. 203–6.

Index of Artists

Balen, Hendrik van   12
Beuckelaer, Joachim   16
Bloemen, Pieter van   20
Boeyermans, Theodor   22
Borcht, Hendrik van der   26
Bril, Paul   30
Brueghel the Elder, Jan   32
Brueghel the Younger, Jan   12
Brueghel the Younger, Pieter   36
Cleve III, Hendrik van   42
Cossiers, Jan   44
Foucquier, Jacques   46
Francken III, Frans   94
Francken the Younger, Frans   50, 60
Fyt, Jan   54
Gossaert, Jan   56
Govaerts, Abraham   60
Grimmer, Abel   64
Heem, Cornelis de   68
Horemans the Younger, Jan Josef   70
Hulst I, Pieter van der   76
Huys, Pieter   78
Kessel the Elder, Jan van   82
Key, Adriaen Thomas   86
Massys, Quentin   88
Monogrammist IHB   92
Neeffs I, Pieter   94
Pourbus the Younger, Frans   98
Quellinus II, Erasmus   82
Rijckaert, Marten   102
Roore, Jacques Ignatius de   104
Rubens, Peter Paul   108
Snijers, Peeter   112
Soens, Jan   114
Son, Joris van   118
Teniers the Younger, David   122
Thulden, Theodor van   140
Unidentified Artist   128
Veen, Otto van   132
Veerendael, Nicolas van   136
Vos, Cornelis de   138
Vos, Paul de   140